Canoeing
the
Congo

Canoeing
the
Congo

First source to sea descent of the Congo River

PHIL HARWOOD

Matador
5 Weir Road
Kibworth Beauchamp
Leicester LE8 0LQ, UK
Tel: (+44) 116 279 2299
Fax: (+44) 116 279 2277
Email: books@troubador.co.uk
Web: www.troubador.co.uk/matador

ISBN 978 1780880 075

British Library Cataloguing in Publication Data.
A catalogue record for this book is available from the British Library.

Typeset by Troubador Publishing Ltd, Leicester, UK
Printed and bound in Great Britain by TJ International Ltd, Padstow, Cornwall

Matador is an imprint of Troubador Publishing Ltd

For Mum and Dad

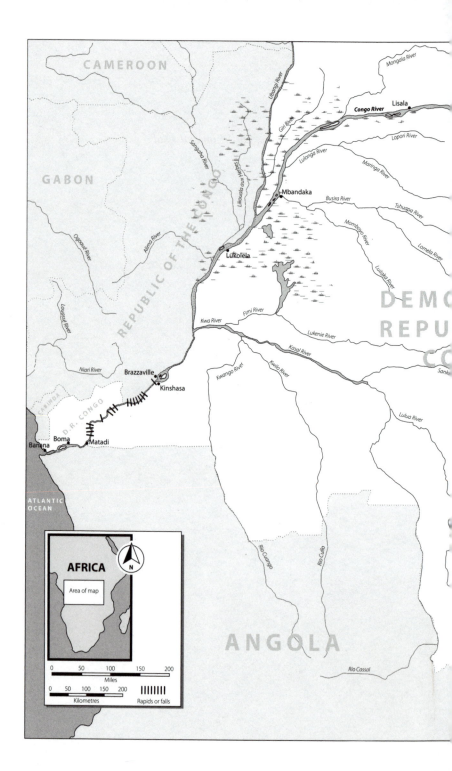

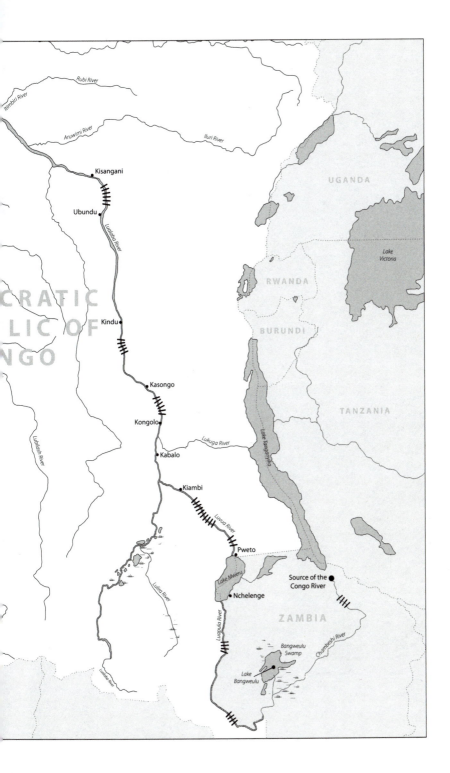

CONTENTS

Foreword   xi

Preface   xiii

Why The Congo?   1

The Six P's: *Prior Preparation and Planning Prevents Poor Performance*   11

In Search Of The Source: *Bureaucracy on a Stick*   20

The Chambeshi: *Crocodiles and Catapults*   33

Bangweulu Swamp: *Dr Livingstone, I Presume*   45

The Luapula: *Bandits and Waterfalls*   61

Lake Mweru: *Tanks and White Caps*   77

The Luvua: *Uncharted Territory*   91

The Middle Lualaba: *Malaria, Chased and Arrested*   109

The Lower Lualaba: *Death Threats in the Abattoir*   151

Kinshasa: *The Atlantic Ocean or Bust*   180

Epilogue   202

Appendix   206

FOREWORD

I first met Phil Harwood when he came to the Winston Churchill Memorial Trust for his Fellowship interview to become a Churchill Fellow. When we heard his proposal for an expedition to canoe down the Congo, we could only assume that he must be slightly mad! After all a civil war still raged in the country, he had no planned back up or communications, and seemed completely nonplussed when we pointed out that his chances of not returning were rather high.

We soon realised that Phil was not only a tough and determined ex Royal Marine, but a very experienced canoeist, outdoor instructor and expedition leader, who had planned his trip in great detail. His proposal was a challenge in the finest tradition of British exploration, completely unconstrained by today`s increasingly restrictive "Health and Safety" mentality, and one that we felt that Sir Winston would have entirely approved of.

Phil did not let himself or us down, and this book is the wonderful story of his journey, which was extremely dangerous at times, not only in the finest "Boys Own" tradition, but more topically an example to us all as to what can be achieved with common sense, determination and a spirit of adventure. Phil has spent many years helping others to challenge themselves and develop their skills through his work with Outward Bound and with the Fairbridge Trust. This book I hope will inspire many more people to reach out of their comfort zone, both physically and mentally, and see what can be achieved when they challenge themselves and give free rein to their sense of adventure.

Jamie Balfour
Director General
The Winston Churchill Memorial Trust

PREFACE

I was alone in the middle of deepest, darkest Congo. Worse still, I was being chased by eight angry tribesmen in two dugout canoes – and they were gaining on me.

"Mazungu … Mazunguuu," came the bloodcurdling screams. "Give us money." They were all standing up and paddling like men possessed. The nearest guy had a huge machete attached to his waist.

"Jesus Christ. What the hell am I doing here?" I muttered to myself.

For the past half hour I had been paddling as though my life depended on it. *As though?* It did depend on it. I was praying they would give up the chase, but it was no good. Despite my best efforts they were catching me.

All of my senses were straining at the leash. I couldn't have felt more alive and in the moment - the rhythmic sound of my paddle pulling hard and clean in the water, the heavy pungent aroma of steaming vegetation, the feel of my heart pounding, and the sweat dripping off my nose. The fear was rapidly growing within me, demanding an answer to the age-old question: fight or flight?

★ ★ ★

During my journey I'd come to understand that the amount of trouble I encountered was directly proportional to the size of the village. Give me a hard working humble fishing village any day. In the smaller places, people were generally far too busy trying to feed their kids to worry about the bald white bloke and his fat wallet. But the bigger the place got, the more chance there was of encountering madmen hell bent on making my life a misery. Kasongo was a very big village.

Not long before I was set upon, when the dawn mist still lingered over the water, I had tried to sneak past without attracting attention, hugging the opposite bank. But just when I thought I'd got by safely, I came upon a group of men lingering by the riverside just ahead of me. It quickly became apparent that they weren't in the mood to make a new friend. They burst into life with a suddenness and ferocious intensity that made me wince.

I'd known I was in trouble almost immediately. It wasn't unusual for people to shout for money from the banks, but my gut instinct, which I had come to love and cherish, told me that this time it was different. These guys were just more hostile and aggressive than normal, and they'd made no bones about what they were after. They wanted my money or my life. I tried to introduce myself in my usual polite way but they didn't give me a chance. They just ran into the water and tried to grab my canoe, some of their faces screwed up in pure hatred. It was time to put the power on and get the hell out of there.

Within seconds, I heard the cry "Mazungu" - white man. It was being screamed and repeated along both banks at an alarming rate. It was disconcerting, to say the least. I felt like a wolf that had inadvertently strolled into a farming community and was being hunted down. I had to go faster.

★ ★ ★

I'd spent the last three months of paddling eight to ten hours a day. I was a canoeing machine and confident I could out-paddle most mortals. But now, after paddling my heart out to the point of near exhaustion, I turned around and saw the nearest dugout canoe was less than twenty metres away. So close that I could see the whites of the men's eyes and their teeth bared in a contorted, hate-filled travesty of a smile.

For the first time on my long journey, I wished that I had bought the handgun I'd been offered in Pweto. If I'd had that, I could have fired a couple of shots in the air and maybe scared these guys off. But now? I couldn't believe this was happening. Why did they hate me so much? What was it going to be: roll over and expose my soft underbelly, or put up a fight? It was the venom in the next cry of "Mazungu" that made me decide. I grabbed my machete.

WHY THE CONGO?

My friend Pat and I were sitting out on our newly built patio behind our tent in the middle of the desert in the north of Iraq in 1991. Earlier on that day, we'd stumbled across an abandoned marble factory while on patrol and taken quite a liking to a pile of rather expensive looking paving slabs. Now, established on our makeshift extension, watching the sun go down and drinking tea, we were discussing what to do when we left the Marines. After much deliberation, we came to the conclusion that driving a Land Rover across Europe and Africa, from London to Cape Town, should be a cracking adventure.

The idea caught hold. A few years later, in 1994, we were ready for the off. We had thirteen thousand miles and twenty-one countries ahead of us and the only thing holding us back was the fact that we had to push our twenty-year-old Land Rover to get it started. When we were swearing at the thing on my Mum's driveway, its failure to fire into life seemed like a bad omen for the trip to come – but once the engine fired, and we were roaring down the road, it went like a dream. We had no trouble for almost the entire journey – unless you count a punch up in Gibraltar, nearly blowing ourselves up crossing a minefield, getting lost in the Sahara desert and encountering armed bandits. Really, it all seemed to go relatively smoothly. Okay, between us we also caught malaria, hookworm, ringworm, schistosomiasis and typhoid – but those were mere issues. It was the trip of a lifetime.

And the highpoint of that trip, as far as I was concerned was the Democratic Republic of the Congo – or Zaire, as it was known back then. I'll never forget my first sight of the Congo itself, in

1

Kinsangani, where locals call it "the river that swallows all rivers." I saw something special in its dark waters. It was like a quietly brooding beast, all mighty, yet momentarily at peace. All the stress of the long journey I'd taken to get there melted away. As I sat mesmerised watching large clumps of water hyacinth float lazily by, the hairs on the back of my neck stood out. I was starting to imagine what it might be like to canoe the river from source to sea. The seed of another idea had been planted. This time, it only took fourteen years to come to fruition…

★ ★ ★

Zaire more than lived up to its wild reputation, but it was the desperate poverty and raw honesty that had the most profound effect on me. I don't think I've ever been the same since – in a good way. My psychiatrist might tell you otherwise, but what the hell does he know?

Driving through Zaire was frustrating, exhausting, liberating and empowering, in that order. But it was frustrating in a good way, because for the first time in my life, I was forced to improvise, to think out of the box and most importantly to rekindle dormant instincts that are rarely required in the western world. We had to live by our wits and slowly strip away all that our consumer society tells us should be important.

I had known we were going to be in for one hell of an adventure from day one, when we tried to cross over the Oubangi River border from the Central African Republic. At the crossing point, we had to find the ferry ourselves. The place was deserted, so we paddled ourselves in a dugout canoe across the sluggish brown river, where we discovered the rusting ancient hulk of what looked like a derelict 'second world war' pontoon craft. There were no vehicle tracks, no officials and no soldiers. The only sign of humanity was an overgrown footpath heading off into the steaming thick jungle. (This turned out to be the main road.) Eventually, a lone man wandered out of the forest and set the tone for the next few weeks.

His first words were: "Two hundred dollar, I take you across river."

Ours were: "You're having a laugh my friend. Think again."

Three hours of haggling later and we finally agreed on ten dollars, at which point the guy told us the pontoon didn't work, and even if it did, he didn't have any fuel. So we canoed back and forth carrying car batteries and diesel trying to get it started. Finally we had to turn an oversize crank handle deep in the engine room, while standing ankle deep in god knows what. We emerged successful but soaked in oil and sweat. It felt like something out of the film *The African Queen*. And I loved every minute of it. I was hooked.

★ ★ ★

The main thing that struck me back in 1994 – and struck me just as forcefully on my more recent trip – was the ingenuity and courage of the Congolese people. The government didn't seem to give a damn about its citizens in the rain forests, but still they survived and often flourished, showing amazing resilience in the face of dreadful conditions.

I've since worked as an overland expedition leader all over Asia, the Middle East and Africa. But never have I experienced roads like I did in the Congo, and I use the word 'road' in the loosest possible sense. Even with a four-wheel-drive we struggled to make progress. There were holes so deep you could often step from ground level onto the roof rack. Water was constantly coming over the bonnet and in through the doors. We were always using shovels to dig ourselves out of the mud, and axes to chop our way through fallen trees. It was one thing after another and never got any easier. Most of the bridges were made from colossal trunks straddling the river below, often with a huge gap in the middle. This was fine if you had a big truck, but not so great in a tiny Land Rover. It meant one slip and we were off. The general rule was you never drove at night, but sometimes it was a choice of either camping next to armed drunks or heading off into the darkness. And when only half of each wheel was touching each log, at night in the middle of a rainstorm, it was literally touch and go.

There were plenty of daytime challenges too. Once, as we were hurtling along a rare piece of decent dirt road in the middle of nowhere, a soldier suddenly jumped out of the jungle and stood in the middle of the track. He confidently put his hand up and ordered us to stop, his other hand covering the pistol on his belt.

I would have loved to do as he asked, and I would have done it too, if it hadn't been for the fact that we had no brakes at that point. I stamped continuously on the pedal with no effect, but we just kept going. I'll never forget the look of horror on his face as he realised he was about to be run over, and hurled himself like a goalkeeper in full flight for the safety of the trees. On went the hand brake and we skidded to a halt, just as we heard what sounded like a gunshot from behind. The cloud of dust in our wake slowly revealed the silhouette of our understandably angry soldier. He was in a full shooting stance, pointing his gun in our general direction. Transforming into diplomatic mode and explaining our lack of brakes, we soon had him eating out of the palm of our hands and he eventually put his 'bad-boy' back in it's holster.

Our next encounter was even more memorable: it was a guy trundling along the road on a homemade wooden bike, complete with solid wooden wheels. He'd carved the thing from the materials he found in the forest, using a machete, and bound it together with strips of rubber inner tube. It was a work of art. This bloke had been pushing the heavily loaded bike uphill and riding downhill for two weeks, sleeping in the jungle at night, just to sell his goods for a profit of twenty dollars. After that he'd make his way back to repeat the process. The dead monkey he had strapped to his handlebars was his only food, and he even tried to sell us that.

Meeting the guy with the wooden bike on his Herculean task and seeing the strength of character and wisdom in his eyes, put everything into perspective for me. I realised that there is no education like adversity.

On a survival course ten years earlier, I'd seen the same look in the eyes of the legendary Lofty Wiseman. Lofty had spent twenty-six years in the S.A.S and by all accounts, he was a ruthless killer. But when he made me a cup of tea in his kitchen, whilst getting some locusts and an un-plucked pheasant out of his fridge, that wasn't how I saw him. He was one of the funniest, friendliest blokes you could ever hope to meet, and his eyes spoke, not of turmoil, but contentment and inner peace. I learnt how to shoot a rabbit in the balls at a thousand yards on that course, but it was Lofty's positive influence that really helped me. That was worth its weight in gold. He was an inspiration.

What Lofty and the man on the wooden bike had in common was a lifetime of exposure to adversity and fear, and it made them the men they were. One of them went looking for it by choice, and the other was born into it, in a country without effective government that was exploited by foreign powers, plagued by war and corruption, and where 'survival of the fittest' was the order of the day. Either way I wanted the qualities that these guys shared; qualities that money can't buy. I hoped the Congo would give me the opportunity to develop them.

Obviously, innocent victims of war and famine (amongst other things) would argue against willing exposure to adversity, and rightly so. But for those of us who feel we are victims of comfort… Well…

* * *

I poured over maps and accounts of the region on my return from Africa, gradually working out a plan and a route.

At 2922 miles long, the Congo is Africa's second longest river after the Nile and the eighth longest on the planet. Its flow rate is the second most powerful in the world, after the Amazon, discharging 1,500,000 cubic feet of water per second. It's also the deepest river in the world, reaching depths of 750ft. It rises in the highlands of North Eastern Zambia at an elevation of 5,760 feet and at a distance of about 430 miles from the Indian Ocean. Its course then takes the form of a gigantic counter clockwise arc, with numerous rapids and waterfalls along the way. It flows through savannah, swamp and dense tropical rainforest, crossing the equator twice before finally draining into the Atlantic Ocean at the village of Banana. Such is the force of the river there at the coast, that fresh water can still be found two hundred kilometres out to sea.

Charting my course wasn't as simple as just getting to one end and paddling to the other. For a start, I had to be sure where the start was. There are three main tributaries of the Congo: the Lukuga River (an outlet of Lake Tanganyika), the Lualaba River (which is said to have the greatest volume and was originally thought of as the source of the Congo), and the Chambeshi River (the latter being the longest and having its source in Zambia).

I decided that to do a true full descent, I would have to paddle from the source of the Chambeshi, in Zambia, down through the Bangweulu swamps, which then flow into and form the Luapula River, which in turn flows into the vast Lake Mweru. I would follow that until it drained into the Luvua River, and follow the Luvua into the Lualaba. This mass of water then flows all the way to the Atlantic Ocean.

Various people have navigated lower sections of the Lualaba.

Henry Morton Stanley was the first to explore the middle and lower-river, following the Lualaba from Nyagwe to the Atlantic Ocean in 1877. He started from Zanzibar on the East coast, and the entire journey took him a neat 999 days. Of the original 356 men on his expedition, only 114 made it to the end. The last remaining European besides Stanley drowned on the final set of rapids, prompting Stanley to write, "I am weary, oh so weary, of this constant tale of woes and death." Perhaps unsurprisingly, he came under much criticism from the establishment on his return, for the ruthless way in which he had conducted the expedition.

On the centenary of Henry Morton Stanley's trans-African expedition, in 1975, John Blashford Snell led a very successful Army expedition from the source of the Lualaba River to the Ocean. The one hundred and sixty strong international team of medical experts, biologists and soldiers used special jet craft, inflatable rafts and scout planes to follow the river all the way to the Atlantic. They even ran most of the rapids on the lower section below Kinshasa, and I believe it took them approximately three months.

Apart from the rapids below Kinshasa, I was planning to do that – and more – by myself. As far as I know after years of research, no one has made it all the way from the Chambeshi source to the Ocean. Mine was to be the first descent from the true source.

★ ★ ★

Paddling all that way was going to be hard – but there were even bigger challenges ahead of a different kind. The Democratic Republic of the Congo has been called 'the world's largest failed state' and 'the most dangerous country on earth for women and children.' You could argue it's one of the few countries in the world that has gone backwards in the last fifty years. Certainly, it has economically. Although that's not to say the years before the previous half century were much happier. The Congo has suffered horribly throughout its history – and generally powerful outside interests have been directly to blame. It is a story of international exploitation, corruption, war and criminal enterprise.

King Leopold II of Belgium was the first – and arguably the worst – European leader to exploit the people of the Congo, taking control of the country back in 1885. It would be Belgium's first colony. He called it the Congo Free State – ironically enough, since he was in complete control. These were dark times for the indigenous population. Locals were forced to produce rubber or die, and countless horrific atrocities were committed in the name of his gluttonous blood stained ambition. Fear was used as motivation. A common punishment for not producing enough rubber was to cut off the right hand, not just of men, but women and children too. Over a twenty-year period, before he was eventually forced to relinquish power to the Belgian State, Leopold turned the country into a vast labour camp.

Things got better when the Belgian State took over – but not much better. Forced labour remained, as did the exploitation of the country's mineral wealth and widespread repression. There was some economic development and improvements in the infrastructure after World War II – but it was too little too late. In 1960, DR Congo finally gained independence from colonial rule. The hero of the people Patrice Lumumba was democratically elected as the new Prime Minister. During his speech at the Independence Day celebrations, he passionately denounced the harsh brutalities and indignities suffered under Belgian rule – but that didn't do him any favours. The Belgians had been helping the Americans get hold of uranium from Congolese mines to manufacture their first atomic weapons. The last thing the US wanted was for this resource to fall into the hands of the Soviets. It shouldn't be taken as too much of a coincidence, therefore, that Patrice Lumumba was assassinated within a year coming to power. Congolese accomplices and a Belgian execution squad were used to carry out the deed, but the CIA were also rumoured to be right behind it.

It was also thanks to US backing that General Mobutu seized power in 1965. Mobutu quickly revealed himself to be a ruthless ego maniac, who at one stage forbade the mention of anyone's name apart from his own in the media (people were identified only by the positions they held), used torture as a political weapon and gave most of the best jobs in government to members of his own tribe. In 1972 he changed his name to Mobutu Sese Seko Kuku Ngbendu Wa Za Banga, which roughly translates as "The Great Unstoppable Warrior Who Goes From Victory To Victory." He obviously hadn't let the power go to his head then. He also ran the country's economy like his personal piggybank, hoarding millions in foreign bank accounts till his demise in 1997. The net result of his rapacious folly was that the country was left with a virtually non-existent infrastructure. There are roughly one hundred thousand miles of roads, but only fifteen hundred of those are paved – and most of those are in and around the capital of Kinshasa. There is no health or education service outside the main cities, telephone lines don't exist, nor is there a postal service. Officials and soldiers alike are rarely paid, and so unsurprisingly it has become one of the most corrupt countries in the world.

It's also a country that has been ravaged by war. The Great War of Africa began in the Congo in 1998, involved eight separate countries (and more than 25 different armed groups) and by the time it ended in 2003, left millions dead. Salvatore Balamuzi, a member of the Lendu community, became an unwilling representative of the conflict when the loss of his parents, two wives and five children led him to say:

I am convinced now, that the lives of the Congolese people no longer mean anything to anybody. Not to those who kill us like flies, our brothers who help kill us, or those you call the international community... Even God does not listen to our prayers anymore and abandons us.

★ ★ ★

By the time I was due to visit in 2008, it was two years after the first democratic elections in forty-six years, and there was peace in the vast majority of the country. There were still plenty of frightening

9

stories about the region – but I didn't want to succumb to scare mongering. I wanted to see for myself.

Despite its terrible history, I love the Congo. I find the people an absolute inspiration. We could all learn a lot from their courage and resilience. They also seem a lot more cheerful and content than we are. Maybe we have too many choices in the West. Like kids in a sweet shop, we get greedier by the minute looking at all the things on offer, and ever more annoyed because we can't have it all. As I sit here now, writing this book in Bermondsey, inner city London, all I can hear are police sirens, there's a drunk curled up asleep on my doorstep, and everybody's got a pit-bull.

THE SIX P'S:

*Prior Preparation and Planning
Prevents Poor Performance*

As a kid I found myself drawn to canoes, probably because I was an ugly bastard and had no confidence with girls. It certainly wasn't because of the appeal of the concrete banked River Crouch, which ran through the middle of my hometown of Wickford in Essex. This was not a particularly enticing river and had more than its fair share of shopping trolleys and discarded bikes. Yet, after a heavy downpour even this boring, pathetic little stream transformed into a raging torrent. Then it became worthy of exploration. We had some great adventures – my mates in a rubber dingy and me in my canoe. Often at night and without life jackets. Ignorance was bliss.

My love of canoes took me into the Royal Marine Commandos. The five years I spent with them was probably the making of me – although I didn't exactly follow the path I intended. It was also canoes that led me astray. My intention had been to join the prestigious 'Mountain and Arctic Warfare Cadre', but my application was thrown in the bin. I was deemed irresponsible after a supposed reckless evening soirée. My friends and I were arrested for abseiling two hundred feet off the motorway Tamar suspension bridge in Plymouth at night. A train spotter walking his dog saw us abseiling down into an inflatable canoe, thought we were up to no good and called the police. We got community service on Dartmoor for that one.

Still, I was toughening up and getting to know a few things. Serving in Arctic Norway and the Jungles of Borneo taught me how to look after myself in extreme environments, while a few months in Iraq taught me that the Americans have got a lot more money than we have.

After that, it was Africa and the beginning of my dream of canoeing down the Congo. It took me a long time to get there, but in that time I still followed my love of adventure and challenge, working as a personal development instructor for Outward Bound in Wales. Most people think Outward Bound is a generic name for all outdoor courses, but the organisation itself has very specific aims. Outward Bound was founded by Kurt Hahn during World War II to provide extremely challenging outdoor courses to toughen up young sailors, because when the younger seamen had found themselves bobbing around in lifeboats, they didn't survive as well as their older counterparts – hence the need for life changing experiences, that would toughen them mentally and physically. The essence of Outward Bound's philosophy was summed up in Kurt Hahn's favourite saying:

We are all better than we know. If only we can be brought to realise this, we may never again be prepared to settle for anything less.

I learned a lot about myself in my time with Outward Bound. Every week I'd be teaching Hahn's values and telling groups things like, "only by getting out of your comfort zone, will you experience growth," and the old favourite, "the only way you'll conquer fear is to face it," and I was forced to admit a home truth to myself. I hadn't yet paddled the Congo because I was scared. Probably more scared of failure than anything else – although death didn't exactly feature high up there on my 'to do' list.

One day on top of our local mountain, Cadair Idris, basking in glorious sunshine and looking out over a sea of clouds below (thanks to a rare temperature inversion), I found inspiration and made a long overdue commitment: I was going to paddle the Congo in 2008. No excuses; grant or no grant. It was time to get busy.

The first job was to pay for the trip. I sent off dozens of letters asking for sponsorship, and applied to every organisation offering grants I could find – but got nothing back. Finally in December 2007, I was asked to come for an interview at the Winston Churchill Memorial Trust Headquarters in London. I had applied for a grant for the previous two years in the 'Adventure and Exploration' category but hadn't made it to this stage, so I was chuffed to bits that my perseverance had paid off. I would finally get a chance to sell the Congo expedition and myself to the panel of four, which included the Director General Jamie Balfour, and travel writer and renowned photojournalist Nick Danziger.

The interview was initially pretty tough, but when they said I'd probably die and called me mad, I suggested that Nick Danziger's travels across Afghanistan during the Russian invasion weren't exactly sensible. Things started to go my way after that. I was awarded a travelling fellowship and grant for which I will be eternally grateful.

I now had four months to make my final preparations, as I wanted to start the expedition in the middle of May 2008. The watershed for the Congo River is so vast that it has two distinct rainy seasons. South of the equator it's between October and May. I wanted to time the trip so I had enough water to paddle the smaller Chambeshi River and the Bangweulu swamps, but not too much water for when I got to the rapids of the Luapula and Luvua Rivers. Either way I was delighted I had won the fellowship, and barring death, blindness or man-flu, I was now confident my dream would soon become a reality.

★ ★ ★

Next on the list was a canoe. I spent many hours thinking about the pros and cons of all the different types of Canadian canoes I could take, and finally decided on a 15ft long 'Mad River Explorer.' It was made from Royalex plastic and was tough as old boots, yet at 20kg was light enough for me to able to carry by myself. It was also short enough to be manoeuvrable on white water, yet long enough to maintain speed on the flat sections. (In case you're not sure, a Canadian canoe is open topped, easy to get in and out and with lots of room for your kit.)

A dugout canoe would have been the other alternative. They're great on the flat and on easy rapids, but when you've got rocks to dodge, and bigger rapids with waves breaking into the boat, they're not so effective. Dugouts are heavy enough as it is, but when half full of water they're virtually uncontrollable and can easily sink. Carrying them around a waterfall is impossible when you're on your own because they're so heavy. Another disadvantage with dugouts, is that they're too heavy to pull up to any camping ground set back from the river at night. If you leave them by the river, they can easily get stolen, but camping next to them by the bank is not always practical, especially when there is a chance of rain and flooding.

Kayaks, meanwhile, are the perfect white water river craft (if you're highly skilled). They also have the added advantage that if someone tries to rob you, you can pick a kayak up and smash them over the head with it. But on a five-month solo trip, the disadvantages heavily outweigh the advantages. Firstly, to paddle serious rapids in a kayak, you really need other kayakers so you can back each other up with safety ropes and rescues if something should go wrong. They're also very slow on flat water, and leave you bugger all room to put all your kit – especially your food.

Once I'd selected my canoe, I thought long and hard about how to prepare it for the Congo, my main concern being security.

My first job was to rivet a steel plate to the bow. I passed a steel cable through it, along with a combination bike lock, so that I could attach the boat to a tree if I had to leave it. Central African machetes are lethal when used on flesh, but they're pretty poor for any heavy chopping of wood, let alone metal.

I also added customised foam blocks at either end of the canoe, which created hidden compartments underneath. These were locked into position with two ten-litre plastic jerry cans one end (for water), and a twenty-litre food barrel the other end. They were both lockable with more wire cable. The two pieces of hard foam would also act as my bed when moved together, keeping me off the floor and away from any creepy crawlies. Should I capsize in rapids, the foam would also help to keep the canoe afloat and buoyant, and – in conjunction with fifteen feet of floating rope I had attached to either end – enable me to climb back in without losing the canoe.

And that was it, the ultimate expedition canoe, ready for hell or high water. Built in Canada, customised in Essex, it would be flown halfway around the world costing me a bloody fortune, before finally losing it's expedition virginity in the Congo, the Heart of Darkness.

★ ★ ★

Next up was equipment, and as far as I was concerned the less stuff I had the better. Is it me, or are we all a bit obsessed with the need to buy expensive outdoor kit? When travelling in Third World countries, part of my enjoyment is to live as simply as I can handle. As much as anything else, doing so gives you more empathy with the local people, breaks down barriers, helps build a rapport and gains respect. And, it's cheaper.

Why spend a fortune on a fancy ceramic water filter, when you can strain river water through your clothing and add a drop or two of iodine? Boiling is always an option, but it's a right old faff, and takes far too long.

Why buy an expensive cooker and hard-to-find fuel, when you are surrounded by firewood most nights? Everybody loves to stare into a fire, and if it rains, hunger is a great motivator for improving your fire-lighting skills.

Why lie huddled in your tent, oblivious as to what's happening outside, when you could be watching the sunset, sensing the changes as darkness falls, and night and its critters reveal themselves, and then gazing up at the stars? My preferred sleeping system in hot climates is a small tarpaulin combined with a mosquito net, and I set it up in a way that gives me 360 degree vision all around. This way, if anyone or anything then tries to sneak up on me, I've got more chance of seeing them and taking pre-emptive action. Night-time is the time for wildlife, and on a previous trip I had come face to face with a clouded leopard using this rig. You don't always need the tarp of course, but since I've had malaria before, I knew the mosquito net was a must. It would also keep out my biggest fear: spiders! I once woke up and a Tarantula was crawling across the net above my face. God I loved that net.

Why also take expensive western food, when you're sitting on top of a river full of fish? I took tinned sardines and rice bought locally for when there were no people about, and then topped it up along the way, buying fresh, dried, salted or fried fish from the local fishermen on route. I did take fishing kit with me, but soon realised I needed to spend virtually every daylight hour paddling, and ended up giving it all away.

In short, less is more.

Other equipment I took included a substantial medical kit, with plenty of antibiotics, even if I couldn't find a tablet for the 'Ebola virus' (the last outbreak of which occurred in 2007). I also planned to make a film documentary of the trip (my first), so I took a Canon HF10 HD film camera, a tripod and a Canon Powershot A650 IS compact camera, all packed nicely away in a waterproof Peli Case. To make everything look less expensive, I used a permanent black marker pen, and masking tape to cover all the shiny silver bits. When I had finished, they looked like something you would buy in a boot sale for fifty pence. Ideally I wanted the locals to think I was a tramp and feel sorry for me, not see me as an international playboy bearing gifts.

★ ★ ★

Another important preparation I had been working on over the years, was people skills.

Previous trips and the characters I had met had taught me a hell of a lot about conflict management.

I received a great lesson on my London to Cape Town trip. It was after dark close to the Liberian border, when we were stopped by an armed drunken mob. The guy in charge, whisky bottle in one hand, and gun in the other, put the barrel of his rifle through my window, pointing it at my head.

"Get out, get out … we are taking your vehicle," he screamed angrily shaking his rifle to emphasise the fact that he meant business. I hoped he wouldn't shake it too hard and accidentally pull the trigger. My first instinct was to smile and offer to shake his hand, so I held out my hand. This only made him angrier and he again shouted for us to get out. But there was something in his eyes that said to me he was bluffing, a look of doubt and guilt – a tiny chink in his resolve.

"I am sorry but we cannot do that, my friend has malaria and I must take him to hospital immediately," I lied spontaneously. Pat quickly got the hint and played dead, complete with moaning, groaning sounds.

"Okay then give us money. US dollar," he backtracked shouting not quite so loudly. Some of his cronies joined in: "American dollar. Give us."

"I'm sorry, but our money was stolen yesterday," I said, starting to blossom as a liar. "We must go to the bank in the next town," I continued.

The poor bloke looked totally dejected, but I wasn't exactly oozing sympathy at this point. Half an hour later we came to a compromise.

"Take these tablets, they will make you very strong. They are very good for you," I finally suggested, handing him our parting gift. We shook hands and waved our goodbyes. They were laxative tablets. It served him right for sticking a gun in my face – sucker!

Another time in Nigeria, a couple of guys simply jumped out into the road with shotguns and face masks and held up their hands for me to stop. I slowed down initially before accelerating into them at the last second, and they were forced to dive out of the way.

My scariest lesson came whilst taking an overland group through Baluchistan, in Southern Pakistan. We had stopped for a pee in the middle of the desert. Girls were on one side of the truck and guys on the other, and out of nowhere a Land Cruiser full of armed Afghanis turned up. A guy then jumped out, walked right up next to me, and started firing his AK47 indiscriminately into the desert. He then turned to me, stuck the barrel of his rifle forcefully into my stomach and stared wildly into my eyes. I noticed he hadn't put the safety catch on which wasn't good, but what worried me most was his crazy spaced-out look. He had clearly been smoking something that rhymed with podium. There was a lot of drug smuggling in this area. Again I smiled and stuck out my hand, offering to shake his, holding it there... waiting. Both of us just stood there for what seemed like an eternity, staring into each other's eyes. I actually thought he was going to shoot me, but he eventually lowered his weapon, shook my hand and asked for a cigarette.

The moral of these stories for me is this: if in doubt when facing unsavoury characters, stick your hand out and smile, but look strong, stare unblinkingly deep into their eyes and give them the mother of all handshakes. This combined with a 'mess with me and I'll rip your head off' look in your eyes, should give you a fighting chance. Eventually somebody's got to back down – and hopefully it won't have to be you.

★ ★ ★

The last thing I needed to get ready was my head. There are a couple of methods that I've used over the years, and even in a short space of time they have proved to be very effective. If you don't give up, they can rapidly transform you into a behemoth of mental strength, ready to take on the world.

The first method is cold water swimming, and I have to say its one of the most invigorating experiences I can think of. The colder it is, the more invigorating it is. So long as you don't drop dead of a heart attack, you always feel fantastic afterwards. Mind over matter. During the winter preceding the trip, I took every opportunity to 'test my mettle' wherever I could. On one occasion I set my alarm clock for two in the morning and jumped into the local river. Never again.

The next method is boxing. Barbaric to some, an art to others, either way it can also be an excellent way of sharpening your most important tool; your mind. With this in mind I joined a boxing gym in the East End of London for a few months. I got the odd black eye and fat lip (mostly thanks to a pot-bellied Russian lunatic called Boris) but when my head finally stopped throbbing, I believed that I had regained the indomitable spirit of my youth, and was ready for anything.

When May 2008 came around and it was time to leave London, I thought that if I was not ready then, I never would be. I'm sure I had probably forgotten something, but if a Congolese fisherman could survive with a machete and a hard work ethic, then so could I.

IN SEARCH OF THE SOURCE

Bureaucracy on a Stick

I remember once saying to my mum: "Don't worry, I won't do it by myself, that would be suicide." Two years later those words came back to haunt me, when I was sat on a flight to Zambia, on my own.

Ideally I would have loved to go with a good friend. Unfortunately my good friends were either too settled, or didn't share my masochistic tendencies (their words). Meanwhile, the risk of travelling with a stranger on such a long trip is too great. You never really know whether you're going to get on until you go through hard times together. You may end up best of friends. Or, you may end up tying pork chops to the other guy's feet in the hope a crocodile will take him in the night. Or, even worse, he may end up tying them to your feet.

I didn't want to take the risk. At least travelling on your own you get complete freedom to do what the hell you want, when you want. You are also more likely to be accepted by the locals, as you're less of a threat. What's more, I managed to convince myself that I'd get more out of the experience, as it would be more of a challenge going solo.

Touching down in Lusaka was a great feeling. I already had a three-month visa, which was more than enough time to get through Zambia. So I was more than a little disappointed when I was now told along with every other foreigner at the airport, that they would only issue a three-week stamp in my passport. I would then have to extend it at the end of that period. That would have been fine if I was going anywhere other than the middle of a swamp. I tried to be philosophical about the whole thing. It was simply the first obstacle of many that were going to test my resolve on this trip. I just hadn't expected the problems to start five minutes after arrival. I had also hoped to get a six-month Congo visa here. Surely that wasn't too much to ask?

Back in London, The Congolese Embassy had never answered the phone. When I'd finally taken a bus up to Hampstead to find them, I had wondered whether I had the right address. The leafy suburban street didn't strike me as a typical setting for a foreign consulate. When I finally got to the place, sure enough there was a map of the Democratic Republic of the Congo nailed to the front door. The trouble was, it had a jungle for a front garden, complete with abandoned cars, and the ramshackle building looked almost derelict. Unsurprisingly, nobody answered the door.

I didn't fare much better on a spur of the moment visit to the Congolese Embassy in Paris. It had been like a betting shop during the Grand National – which is to say, absolute chaos. There, I eventually worked out that visas were available to foreigners on one day of the week – and that day was the day before I arrived.

Lusaka was my last chance saloon. All the information I'd come across said I could get a visa here. I even wore a shirt and tie to create the right impression, and was the first person at the gate when it opened.

I was nearly blinded as the immigration official arrived. His beaming smile and outrageously colourful shirt lit up the room. It instantly reminded me of my last visit to the Congo, and the local government officials' obsession with loud clothing. I was back. And back in trouble.

"Je voudrais un visa de six mois, s'il vous plait," I said in my best French when he popped his head through the window in the waiting room.

"No problem monsieur, you want a working visa for this six months, yes?" he replied, rummaging through some forms on his desk.

"No, actually I would like a tourist visa."

He stopped what he was doing and glared at me.

"A tourist visa? Have you been to the Congo before?"

He seemed confused.

"I have, many years ago I drove from Bangassou to Kisangani, then into Uganda. Your country is very beautiful monsieur and the people are the most friendly in Africa," I said with a cheesy smile, laying it on nice and thick. He seemed to be lapping it up.

"Where will you enter the Congo my friend?"

He was warming to me, I could feel it. He was under my spell.

"I will cross from Lake Mweru into the town of Pweto," I said as confidently as I could. I noticed his eyebrows raise and his expression change as I said the word Pweto. Alarm bells. Don't panic!

"Pweto? Why do you want to cross into Pweto? There is nothing there. How will you travel on from there? There are no roads. Do you know there is still some fighting there?" he asked, clearly agitated.

I went into an Oscar winning performance that would have made Laurence Olivier proud, doing my level best to win over his confidence. Eventually, after explaining my trip and convincing him I'd be safe, I filled out a form and he told me to come back the next morning to pick up the visa. He was happy, I was happy.

When the doors opened the next morning however, he looked nervous. Somebody just out of sight in a back office, was clearly calling the shots, and telling him to give me some bad news.

"I am very sorry Mr Philip, but we can only give you a two week visa. You can get a six month visa in Pweto." He was looking at the floor, clearly embarrassed.

"Why have you changed your mind? This is the Congo Embassy, if I cannot get one here, how will I be able to get one in Pweto? It's a small town."

I was desperate to persevere, and prepared to beg. Again he looked at the floor occasionally glancing up at his superior, who finally made an appearance.

"We have made our decision, and it is final. You can get a visa in Pweto, or if you want you can travel to Lubumbashi in the Congo."

The superior didn't look like the sort who would change his mind.

"Are you one hundred percent sure I can get one in Pweto?" I asked, pleadingly.

"I am sure," he promised. I thought I'd believe it when I had it in my mitts.

The last thing I wanted to do was travel to Lubumbashi (the Congo's third biggest city). As well as the extra expense, it would take a week or more. So I decided to gamble on Pweto. I didn't want to believe there was still fighting there, but I was told the Mai Mai rebels were stirring up trouble in the area. Fighting or no fighting, I wasn't about to give up just yet.

★ ★ ★

My next job was to cross my fingers and hope my canoe would be waiting for me at the airport freight terminal. Even before I got to reception, I slapped my hands together in celebration. I'd spotted a ridiculously long crate that could only contain one thing. Score!

But before I could pick my precious canoe up, I had to go to a reception office where I met someone called Mr Zulu. He was a man with the power either to help me or make my life hell. He actually – fortunately – turned out to be one of the nicest guys you could hope to meet, even if he was more used to dealing with wealthy businessmen than poverty stricken adventurers.

I didn't know he was such a great bloke on our first meeting, however. In fact, he gave me good reason to suspect the worst. He was mumbling the dimensions of my crate and tapping numbers into his calculator and shaking his head. When he finally looked up, he gave me the good news.

"Okay, here we are Mr Philip, you must pay eleven million Zambian Kwacha for an import permit."

I nearly fell off my chair.

"You must be joking!" I screamed. "It cost me nearly two thousand pounds to fly it out here." Then I got a bit carried away. "I'm not going to pay that in a million years! You could torture me to death, and I still wouldn't pay it. It's too much! How much is that in pounds anyway?"

"Mmmm" he mused, possibly pondering my brainless comment about not paying after I'm dead. He returned to the logic of the calculator. "It comes to about fifteen hundred British pounds."

Bloody hell, surely that couldn't be right. I held my head in my hands. He looked confused. This is when I started to realise he was a nice guy and I was behaving like an idiot. Rather than get angry at my outburst, he had simply become even more humble. About this time, I also noticed the picture of his wife and kids on his desk and I felt like a fool for giving him a hard time. He was only trying to do his job.

As it turned out, after an hour of discussion I realised that in my ignorance I had neglected to apply for a temporary import permit, which would only have come to a hundred quid. When I apologised for my earlier outburst, he asked me if I wanted a free lift back to town on the staff bus. I accepted, feeling suitably chastened.

I returned to the airport the next day for round two. If I hadn't had the letter from the Zambian Tourist Board, I don't think I would have been allowed a temporary import permit. As it was, the wonderful Mr Zulu was prepared to fight my case in front of his not-so-wonderful superior. He looked very nervous before we went into her office and I quickly understood why. Mrs Mugabe (no relation I hoped) looked hard as nails.

"Mr Philip is going to canoe three thousand miles down the Congo River to the Atlantic Ocean," Mr Zulu informed her. Her face didn't crack. She just stared at him in silence.

"He needs a temporary import permit for his canoe." He was starting to sweat. Mrs Mugabe glanced at me, from behind her peeling leather topped desk, still in silence. I was starting to feel sorry for Mr Zulu, poor bloke.

"He is…"

"Mr Philip," she cut him short. "You are not serious, you cannot canoe to the Ocean from here…It is… It is impossible," she finally said. "Where will you leave Zambia?"

"Ah, I'll show you on the map," I said quickly, remembering I had one in my bag. We gathered around her table and I could see the relief on Mr. Zulu's face. I pointed out the Chambeshi and Luapula Rivers flowing into Lake Mweru.

"From here I will leave Zambia at Nchelenge, and import my canoe into the Congo."

"Why do you choose to go to the Congo? It is not safe for you. I cannot allow this. You will be in great danger."

She didn't exactly sound convinced. I showed her my letter and explained my experience. Slowly she started to soften to the point where she seemed malleable enough for me to work my magic. It was time to pull my favourite diplomatic skill out of the bag, reserved for special occasions with the fairer sex … flirting!

"You can come with me if you want. You can look after me, and I will catch a fish for you everyday," I joked, gazing into her eyes with a cheeky smile, trying my best to look handsome.

"I like catfish," she laughed.

"Catfish it is then," I replied. Mr. Zulu started to relax and I knew I had it in the bag. Twenty minutes later, we were done.

I was allowed to go into town to collect the permit that day, but Mr Zulu made me promise I'd phone him when I was about to leave Zambia or he'd be in big trouble. I also found a guy with a pick up truck to take my canoe back to the campsite. I now needed to try to get my Zambian visa extended in town. I was passed from pillar to post, and refused at every point, but I finally got to speak to the boss in the main immigration office. When I was shown inside, something told me my luck had run out. For one thing he looked like a pork pie and was wearing a white suit. Call me judgemental, but the Duran Duran look suggested he was on a power trip and had a big ego. He was extremely overweight, sweating profusely, with a permanent scowl on his face. He also had a steadily deepening furrow in his brow that suggested he thought dealing with a shabbily dressed urchin like myself was way beneath his pay grade.

"What do you want? Why do you come here?" he asked brusquely. "I'm very busy."

He obviously didn't share Mr Zulu's charming qualities, and I struggled to maintain my cheerful demeanour.

"Yes," I said. "I'm actually here to canoe the length of the Congo River, all the way to the Atlantic." He had already lost interest. "And I would like to possibly have a three month visa, as I will be in the middle of Bangweulu swamp when my three week visa expires."

"You can extend your visa in three weeks," he said, already concentrating on his mobile phone more than on me. Either he didn't understand or didn't give a damn.

"But that's the problem," I persevered. "I will be in the middle of the swamp, sleeping in the bush, there will be nowhere to extend it. Do you understand?"

"Of course I understand, I am not stupid", he said furiously.

I was trying to be as polite as possible.

"I'm not …" I tried, but he cut me short.

"Now go! I have wasted enough of my time on you."

I wanted to throw him out the window, but quickly realised he was too heavy. My growing dislike for him was probably written all over my face. It seemed clear he wanted to assert his authority regardless of any logic I might use on him. So I gave up and left. We didn't exchange email addresses. Obviously there would be plenty of hippos and crocodiles on the river who would be only too happy to issue me a visa extension, silly me.

★ ★ ★

26

The nearest town to the source of the Congo River with a train station is Kasama, in the North East of the country. For some reason however, even though Lusaka was the capital city of Zambia, there were no trains leaving the station there (or arriving). But there were trains that went from Kapiri Mposhi a couple of hours drive to the North.

To get there, I employed the services of a local taxi driver called Jason. I already knew Jason was a man I could rely on. I'd met him a couple of days earlier when he'd taken me on one of my many trips to the airport and he'd helped me retrieve some money from another taxi driver who had ripped me off. This guy had claimed to be unable to give me change for a large note, but said he'd come back with it when I needed to be picked up from the airport a couple of hours later. I made the mistake of trusting him – and naturally he didn't show. But when I arrived with Jason the next day, I'd spotted this guy at the taxi rank and asked Jason to stop whilst I jumped out.

"Where's my money?" I asked tapping on the bloke's window.

"Err, err" he was speechless, and then pretended not to remember me. I explained the situation to Jason, and within five minutes I had my money back. After that I'd told Jason about my need to get north and he suggested he borrow his dad's pick up and take me himself. I was starting to like him.

We must have passed about ten police checkpoints on the way to the train station. Seven of them tried to extort some money from Jason, but luckily for me he was as streetwise as they came and they didn't get a penny. It was a classic lesson in the power of confidence. He knew his papers were in order, and he also knew that the police preyed on the nervous and easily intimidated. This knowledge, combined with his laid-back manner, outrageous Hawaiian shirt and cool dude shades, made the cops give up pretty quickly. I was able to soak up the surroundings rather than worry about how much bribe money I was going to have to fork out. The countryside was already pretty different to Bermondsey. It looked as dry as a bone with gentle hills all around that were covered in straw-coloured grass with the odd green-topped acacia tree. Where the potholes were really bad and drivers were forced to slow down, huge bags of charcoal, and boxes of fruit were for sale. Clever stuff.

The red-bricked train station was by far the most impressive building in Kapiri Mposhi, built to last and very well maintained. Best of all, it was full of really helpful staff. Imagine turning up at Paddington station in London with a fifteen-foot plastic canoe in need of help – it would be mayhem, and you'd get charged a fortune. But these guys couldn't do enough for me, and I was soon rattling my way north east, on the twelve-hour overnight train to Kasama. I'd only paid an extra $10 for the canoe. I gazed out of the window breathing in the evening sun, watching the bush unfold, dotted with tiny straw hut villages as far as the eye could see. It felt good to be on my way.

★ ★ ★

Kasama was a sleepy little town, and at over five thousand feet high, had a comfortably cool climate. One of the biggest attractions in the area was its abundance of waterfalls, and the nearby Lake Tanganyika. It also had a decent little supermarket where I started to stock up on rice, and bags of dried kapenta (a tiny local fish), which would last for months.

The day after I arrived I hitched a ride on the Old Great North Road to the village of Masamba, the nearest village to the source of the Chambeshi. From here with the help of Ag, a middle aged rather attractive mother of three and her two side kick young lads, we set off on the back of two bicycles through the bush. After three hours of cycling and walking along numerous trails miles from anywhere, two things were becoming clear to me. One, the amount of work required to live out here, with next to nothing, especially in what was now the dry season, was mind-blowing. Two, I was finding myself increasingly drawn to the sway of Ag's hips. With her equally seductive eyes, I realised she was the most gorgeous guide I had ever met. It was a shame I was soon going to be canoeing away from her.

All the same, it was quite a moment when we finally forced a way through the thick bush in a pocket of lush greenery to get to the source. The tiny spring by a Banyan tree was the start of two thousand nine hundred and twenty-two miles of an incredibly diverse river; the most powerful in Africa. The story goes that the water here takes six months to reach the Atlantic. I hoped to do it in three.

The trickle from the spring was way too small for me to be able to put my canoe in there, so the next day, back in Kasama, I hired Julius, the only guy in town with a 250cc trial bike to take me through the bush in search of the best place to put on. Even though we crashed in soft sand and I thought I'd broken my ankle, we eventually found a decent spot. It was inaccessible by vehicle – even by bike – but I reckoned I could get some help from the nearby village to carry the canoe down.

I'd been camping in the garden of the Thorn Tree Lodge in Kasama, run by an English couple Ewart and Hazel who have been there for thirty-five years. Their daughter Claire, who runs Thorn Tree Safaris, offered to help me out, so the next morning at six o'clock, I left for the upper Chambeshi with her driver, another Julius.

Soon we were out of Kasama and heading north on the badly pot-holed Old Great North Road, passing scores of local women carrying all manner of goods on their heads to sell at Kasama market. After half an hour we were off the tarmac at Nseluka and heading into the bush on dirt tracks. Land cruisers were not uncommon here, but entire villages stopping and staring suggested to me that plastic Canadian canoes were more of a rarity. After an hour of driving through and flattening six-foot high grass, I realised we were getting off the beaten track. Around lunchtime we finally arrived at the tiny village of Chilwe.

In England I had imagined it would be practical for me to carry everything myself in two loads: first carry the canoe on my shoulders, then come back for the food barrel. It was possible, but the reality was that the average daily wage for manual labour in these parts was $3 a day, so I'd have to be a fool not to seek help where available. This way, I'd also be contributing something back to the local people.

Since I'd been here on the trail bike a couple of days previously, however, word had got out about impending arrival and a large, friendly, but noisy crowd soon enveloped our vehicle. I had to jump on the roof and shout for quiet to get things under control. Waving my arms around, I finally got some attention.

"Jambo Habari, I need four people to help carry my canoe down to the river."

Everyone's hand went up.

"Me, me, me!" they all shouted.

I scanned the crowd in confusion, until I noticed one character that stood out from the others. He was a foot bigger than everyone else, built like a brick outhouse and seemed to command respect from the others.

"What's your name?" I asked.

"Patrick," he said.

I stooped down and shook his hand.

"I would like you to be the boss Patrick, I need four people including you. I would like you to pick three others then we can talk money."

"One thousand dollars," he suggested enthusiastically.

"No, no, no, I don't think so. Why don't you find help first and then we'll talk money?"

He turned to face his audience. His beaming smile soon turned into a frown as the crowd erupted and almost swallowed him up, everyone pleading to be picked. He quickly disappeared in a sea of waving arms. I felt a bit guilty, but thought I could pay him a bit extra for his newfound leadership responsibilities.

After arranging a price, meeting the chief and saying my goodbyes to Julius, I set off into the bush with Patrick and his crew. Actually there was an entourage of about twenty, mostly kids, but with at least eight blokes carrying the canoe. I had to stop them and explain to Patrick that I would pay the agreed amount to him only, and he would have to pay the others. This did the trick for a while, but not long after the entourage began creeping in and helping out again. I knew it would end with hassle at the end. But now carrying my rucksack, with my rather heavy food barrel balanced on top of that, I had my own problems keeping up.

After a couple of hours tramping through the bush, we arrived at the headwaters of the Chambeshi River. No more than eight feet wide, the stream looked clean enough to drink there and then, and was flanked by thick bush and long grass. The mid-afternoon sun was warm and I couldn't wait to get paddling. Paying off the guys took a while as they wanted more money, but when I gave my sunglasses to Patrick his contentment seemed to have an effect on the rest. Soon they were waving and cheering as I paddled off.

When I started paddling my way upstream they seemed rather confused, but I was so eager to get on that I had no time for an explanation. I wanted to paddle the Congo River as high up as I could from source to sea, paddling as many rapids possible. I had been to the source itself but it was obviously too small to paddle there. This was the best spot I could get too, but by paddling and poling upstream as far as I could, I would hopefully satisfy myself I had done my best.

After a couple of hours of dragging the canoe through shallows, I was happy I had done enough. "Time for the off!" I shouted to the wilderness. "Atlantic Ocean here I come!"

After 15 years thinking about it and three years planning it, I was finally on my way. I turned and headed downstream. Only two thousand, nine hundred miles to go.

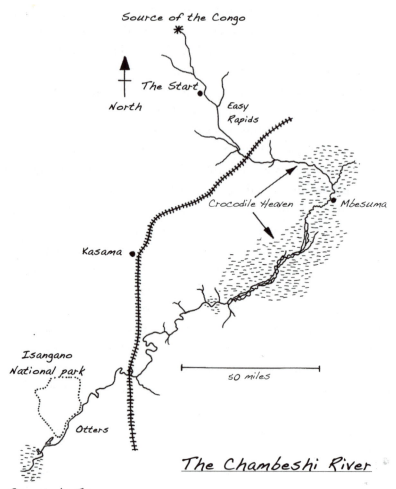

Source of the Congo

North

The Start

Easy
Rapids

Crocodile Heaven

Mbesuma

Kasama

Isangano
National park

Otters

50 miles

The Chambeshi River

Bangweulu Swamp

THE CHAMBESHI

Crocodiles and Catapults

For me, there's something very special about starting a wilderness river journey, especially in a Third World country. Everything becomes clear and uncomplicated, and priorities change. The moneymaking obsessions of the western world melt away and you're left thinking simply about finding food, firewood, shelter, and not drowning.

I knew this would be a dangerous trip, but I was determined to succeed, and the 'fire that burns within' was fierce. I had no kids, no wife, no house and no responsibilities. I had nothing to lose except my life – and something deep within told me that wouldn't happen.

The upper Chambeshi was a beautiful little stream; crystal clear waters, an abundance of birdlife and lovely little rapids to keep me on my toes. Slowly but surely it started widening and the rapids started getting bigger, but never big enough to be life threatening. The only real risks were either being torn to shreds by the razor sharp thorn trees that seemed to lean out over the river from all directions, or getting the canoe pinned against a rock or on one of the many fallen trees crossing the water.

On one occasion I rounded a bend in fast water, only to find myself thrust into a wall of tangled vines and thorns. I was well and truly stuck and only by using my machete did I manage to cut my way through, emerging the other side looking like a scarecrow murderer with blood dripping from his fingers.

Canadian canoes are notoriously easy to get pinned if you're not careful. If you hit an obstacle sideways, and the water pressure from the upstream side pins you against it, you're left unable to move. It gets worse if you tilt or edge the canoe upstream. It then immediately fills with water, the power of which will often wrap the canoe around the obstacle like a piece of paper. This can happen on the easiest of rapids, and, apart from the problems associated with destroying your canoe, if you get your legs caught, you can easily get trapped – with dire consequences. Keeping the canoe pointing downstream is the answer. And all that also explains why one of the golden rules of canoeing and kayaking on rapids is to never go alone.

I was pretty much heading south at this point, not a million miles away from the southern shores of Lake Tanganyika, before the river changed direction and headed east towards Bangweulu Swamp. These first couple of days were an absolute joy, and in the absence of people, each evening I could relax beside my campfire, enjoying the serenity of it all. Although the days were pleasantly warm, the nights were bloody freezing – which was something I hadn't expected. Since looking cool wasn't very high on the priority list, I got into the habit of wearing a pair of boxer shorts on my head, in the absence of a woolly hat.

★ ★ ★

I'll never forget the first guy I met on the river. As I pulled up my canoe to camp one night, he was sitting on a rock cracking open sunflower seeds and wearing a tweed jacket. When he saw me he froze, not unlike a pheasant opting for camouflage rather than movement; on the verge of bolting. He visibly relaxed though as I smiled and waved, and after a few minutes I slowly walked over to say hello. His name was Kabanda.

To say his clothing was in tatters would be an understatement. His jacket was barely holding together and hung off him in long strips. With a thick dishevelled beard, untamed hair and equally

34

wild eyes, he looked like Robinson Crusoe on a bad day. I don't think his feet had ever seen a pair of shoes. He offered me some sunflower seeds, and I invited him over to my canoe and gave him a bag of rice. I thought he was going to cry as he stared at the bag in his hands. He spoke a little English and said he would come back soon. Half an hour later he returned with his three kids, and they awkwardly lined up for my inspection. I did wonder whether these guys lived in a village, as they were clearly in a bad state and looked almost wild.

"Do you have soap?" he asked almost apologetically.

"Just a moment, I have some somewhere," I rummaged around in my canoe. "Here you go," I gave him a large bar I had for washing clothes, thinking it should last for ages.

"How old are your children?" I asked.

He thought for a moment.

"I don't know. Their mother is dead." He stared at them deep in thought. "I had five children, but two died of malaria… I do my best."

The kids ran to the river and had great fun lathering themselves up. Anybody would have thought I had given them a football. I also gave Kabanda some local malaria tablets, and as darkness fell, they wandered off into the bush.

When I'd been surrounded by that same thick bush, and when I was in the rapids, with hills on either side I felt cut off from the outside world, but as the landscape gradually changed, I started coming across the odd fisherman. Now too, I was approaching the Chambeshi flats, a large expanse of swamp, and the meandering bends were long and tedious. After a couple of days I started to realise I was probably paddling three miles from side to side to make one mile in a straight line on the map. Since there were two thousand miles to go, all this became a tad irritating. Occasionally I would notice a tiny gap on a corner which I assumed would allow me to cut off the next bend, and looking carefully at the water would give me clues as to whether it was worth a go. A bit of flow disappearing into the reeds was good, slack water was bad. Sometimes it worked beautifully and I'd save a lot of time and effort, other times it would get thicker and thicker and I'd end up in a mosquito infested hell having to backtrack creating more time and effort. Trial and error taught me a lot.

Some locals would paddle their dugouts out to say hello, others would stand and stare and occasionally they would turn and run. One early morning, I surprised a couple of teenagers in their dugout, and before I could say, "Mulishani" (Bemba for "hello"), they leapt out of their canoes, swam ashore and ran off into the bush. As I shunted their abandoned canoe to the shore I remember hearing the sound of their footsteps gradually disappearing, and realised even Zambia has its wild places, unvisited by the white man.

Crocodiles were another consideration. The closer I got to the bank, and the thicker the swamp, the more chance there was of having a close encounter. Although everybody had warned me about crocodiles and hippos, it was four days until I saw one, and believe it or not, it was actually up in a tree. This was the dreaded 'Zambian tree crocodile' (*crocodilus aerialus*), which would drop from above into your canoe, ram his tail down your throat and use you to scratch his back before ripping your head off. Okay, the six foot croc had actually become tangled in the fallen tree in the recent floods and due to the now receded waters was ten foot off the ground, well and truly dead and very smelly. Not much to worry me – apart from the stink.

A couple of days later however it all got a bit more serious. The environment had now changed again, and where it had once been open and bright, the way became narrow and dark, with gnarled, twisted overhanging trees blotting out the sunlight. As I registered this change in mood and my mind brought up the similarities with the everglades, there was a frenetic thrashing noise to my right. Two twelve-foot crocodiles came crashing through the undergrowth and launched themselves off a four feet high bank. They were so close I remember noticing the membrane close on the nearest one's eyes. They belly flopped onto the water with a tremendous splash and disappeared directly under my canoe, the waves causing me to wobble in more ways than one. I also remember both my eyebrows rising as the crocs hit the water and I imagined their jaws re-emerging and clamping round my head. My heart rate was quite high at that point, and it took me a while to calm down.

After about the tenth crashing croc experience however, I started to realise that they were probably more scared of me than I was of them – at least in a canoe. The locals would hunt them for their meat by boat, when they could. On land it was a different matter, which made selecting a campsite each night more interesting. An unpleasant situation that recurred all too often was when good camp spots were scarce, swamp was all around, dusk was upon me and a big fat croc would make an appearance just before dark. Not good. Paddling on flat water at night is not a big deal, but finding a decent camping ground is. A couple of times I ended up sleeping in my canoe on the water and eating cold food. In the absence of firm ground, my technique would be to paddle as hard as I could, and ram myself into the thickest area of reeds I could find. I'd then try to somehow drag and push my way further through, until I was securely wedged in with little risk of capsize. Up would go my poles and mosquito net, and by moving my two pieces of foam buoyancy together, I could stretch out. Then, depending on how tired I was, I could either be serenaded to sleep, or kept awake all night by the frogs' incessant croaking. I figured that since I was surrounded by tightly packed six feet high reeds, I'd have to be pretty damn unlucky to get a surprise visit from anything big enough to fit my head in its mouth.

On more than one occasion I was awoken in the middle of the night by crashing, splashing sounds, but after a while I got used to it. Crashing, splashing sounds are one thing – something 'orrible ripping your leg off is quite another.

★ ★ ★

I had been on the water about a week now, and was really pleased with the kit I had brought, especially my two, six-foot wooden poles that I had carved to my specifications back in Lusaka. Apart from poking crocodiles in the eye and making an excellent A-frame for my tarpaulin, when used in combination with an empty rice sack, they also acted as an improvised sail if I had the wind behind me. (Which I almost never did.) When I lashed the poles together, the now double length pole also enabled me to stand up and push myself along in shallow water. I used strips of rubber inner-tube (which were universally used in Africa for all manner of things from tying a goat onto your bicycle, to fixing broken vehicle springs) to tie them. And any self-respecting adventurer worth his salt will always have two or three uses for every bit of kit.

★ ★ ★

Mbesuma was a village with a ferry crossing: civilisation. A thriving metropolis compared to everything I'd seen in the previous week.

In East Africa, regardless of local languages, the word Mazungu is generally used for white man. It usually rang out long before I got to the centre of any settlement – and it certainly did today. Mbesuma clearly didn't get many white people visiting, especially arriving by canoe, and amongst the crowd that enveloped me the questions came thick and fast.

"Where's your guide?"

"I have no guide."

"Where do you sleep at night?"

"In the bush."

Gasps all around.

"What about the crocodiles?!"

"I've had no problems so far. Are there many downstream?"

At which point a wrinkled faced old man pushed his head through the crowd and announced: "There's many more crocodiles downstream, and they're much bigger too."

Bloody marvellous, I thought. This guy's name was Thomas and he asked if he could show me around Mbesuma.

"What about my canoe?" I asked. He said something in Bemba to a young man who scuttled off.

"Your canoe will be safe here, don't worry."

As Mbesuma seemed to be a collection of about fifteen huts in a large semicircle I thought I could keep my eye on the canoe. As became the norm, a small friendly crowd gathered around it, rarely touching it but discussing its construction and materials.

"I'm the ferry attendant," Thomas announced. "It is my responsibility to take the cars across."

"How many vehicles cross every day?" I asked.

"Oh, one or two, sometimes none. You must stay here tonight."

"That's very kind but it's very early and I have a long way to go. I'm paddling down the Congo River to the Atlantic Ocean."

His already heavily lined face slowly doubled its wrinkles. "That's impossible, you will be killed," he declared.

"If I take one day at a time, I think it will be possible," I said, patting him on his shoulder. "I would like to buy some food though if you have it?"

"Of course, follow me."

He led me to the largest mud brick shop. If you liked biscuits this was the place to be. I stocked up, gave a couple of packets to Thomas and said my farewells.

"Whatever you do, don't swim in the river!" Thomas shouted as I paddled off.

Sound advice I thought. It reminded me of the old adage: *when travelling, always seek local knowledge.* Doing so had saved my arse a million times over in the past. If in doubt, always ask at least three locals. If two say the same thing, it's a fairly safe bet. If they all say different things, either ask some more people, or it's gut instinct time.

After a couple of days, Thomas's words came back to haunt me. In a particularly beautiful but remote part of the wetlands, after having seen a fair share of crocs that day, I messed up. I had parked up in a reed bed with the intention of doing some filming. As I was struggling to attach the video camera to my little tripod, I inadvertently flicked the battery release switch, and watched in horror as my very expensive battery (one of only three) fell off, bounced on my foam buoyancy and plopped into the water.

NIGHTMARE! I had five months ahead of me with high hopes of making a bestselling documentary film, my solar panel was pathetic and places with power to charge batteries were few and far between. I reached down with my paddle and discovered that the water was only five feet deep. Stripping off naked I lowered myself in, feeling with my feet and toes. The bottom was surprisingly firm and, by tilting my head back, I was just able to breathe. Surely I would find it? Every now and again I'd get shivers down my spine, as my imagination ran amok. I pictured a huge croc creating a bow wave before it exploded from the surface clamping its jaws around my head and shoulders dragging me under. I had my trusty sheath knife on a cord around my neck, and imagined I could ram it into the crocodile's eye socket like they do in the films. I concentrated hard to expel these thoughts, but after half an hour I felt I was pushing my luck and climbed out, unsuccessful. Two batteries and two legs were better than three batteries and one leg.

* * *

That same night camp spots were scarce, as usual. It was reedy all around and there was hardly any dry land about. As I was paddling close to the edge, a huge fat croc, the biggest yet, came crashing out of the reeds and swam right under my canoe. Shortly after this, dusk was upon me and the stars came out. It was a beautiful night. Apart from the occasional thought of crocs, it was actually very pleasant indeed to be there; the frogs were croaking, owls swooping, bats darting and the moon was full enough to illuminate where I was going.

Before too long I heard voices and sure enough I came across a couple of fisherman who luckily spoke pretty good English. I asked if there was any firm land nearby and they invited me to their fishing camp. Half an hour later I was sitting round a campfire chatting to the father of the two fishermen, who turned out to speak excellent English. Peter had served in the Zambian army for twenty-five years. It turned out he came here with his four sons to fish for a few months each year. They seemed to prefer the time after the flood when the receding waters offered better fishing, mostly using gill nets and conical traps. They also dug out trenches in the banks, so when the water dropped, the fish from the flooded surrounding area would head for the trenched channels to be caught like rats in a barrel.

I must admit that I initially felt a little awkward in these situations, since I clearly had so much stuff compared to the people I met. I even felt a little guilty. Tonight, I laid out my roll matt, bivi bag and changed into my dry set of clothes, before finally setting up my mosi net hanging off a fish net drying rack. As they had already eaten, I cooked up my rice on the fire and tucked in with some salted fish I had bought. One of the brothers asked if I had any medicine for his loose teeth – and, indeed virtually every tooth in his mouth moved alarmingly. I gave him some milk powder, and suggested a better diet. Easy for me to say. They had a tiny mud hut which as it transpired was for the father only. The four brothers simply laid down around the fire with a blanket each. I took great care in not revealing my pocket sized down pillow as I tucked myself up in bed.

These were great people, hospitable and friendly, and they never once asked for any money. I gave them a big bag of rice in the morning as thanks and we said our farewells.

The contrasting receptions I received from locals never ceased to amaze me on this trip. It was a lottery – as the next 24 hrs were to highlight. After a peaceful morning with nothing harder to contend with than an inconvenient headwind, I started to encounter more villages. Whenever I paddled close to a village or passed fisherman I'd always say hello and explain myself if I thought they were interested. I was working hard on the local Bemba language and relished any opportunity to practice, even though English was often spoken here in Zambia. I was frequently asked for money, but when I explained I was paddling to the Atlantic Ocean and needed what I had, people usually changed the subject and we would part amicably.

That afternoon however, didn't quite work out so well. I might be an ex-marine, but I'm not totally insensitive. I knew that shouting aggressive locals were often acting up as a result of fear at there being a strange white man in their own backyard. Smiling a lot, explaining myself, being very respectful and trying to shake hands usually did the trick – but today, for some reason, it didn't work with one particularly enraged character.

My suspicions as to his intentions were first aroused, when his first (very loud) words were: "Mazungu! Give me money!"

I paddled close to the shore and did my diplomatic best – but he wasn't having any of it. When he shouted again and tried to wade out to grab my canoe, I backed away, but this just made him even angrier. He was getting into a right old state. Of course I could have given him a couple of dollars and all would have been well, but unfortunately for him and me, I had made a decision early on not to give in to intimidation and not to give money for no reason. Full stop.

Eventually I gave up, but unfortunately as I paddled off, he followed me along the bank, still shouting for money. I put the power on, but he simply started running instead, waving his fist at me. After about twenty minutes the bank started to get very marshy, but he simply ran through it getting more and more agitated. Then, when he was back on firm land, out came the catapult. Why me? I thought that this guy must have some issues, and I doubted there were many psychotherapists available locally.

Twang! He was firing at me. Great! He then came across an empty dugout in the reeds, and sure enough he jumped in and gave chase. Later in the trip I saw this scenario as 'Indiana Jones syndrome' – being chased by angry locals in dugouts. As it was early days, I hadn't yet become the paddling machine I was later, and after twenty minutes it was clear he was catching me up.

I was actually quite scared and felt like a bit of a wimp for being so. It was the first time I'd been chased, he was shouting like a madman (always a bad sign), and I didn't quite know what to do. He may have just been bluffing or he may have wanted to rob me, or worse. The bottom line for me was that I knew it would be worse in DR Congo, and I didn't want to get into the habit of letting fear work against me. I needed to use scary moments to empower me and make me stronger, not turn me into a quivering, gibbering wreck. That was the only way I'd make it to the Atlantic Ocean.

As he came closer I realised I wasn't going to get away so I stopped paddling, stood up and grabbed my machete, laying it on my deck for him to see. I tried some Bemba and asked him what the problem was, but he just stood there and continued shouting. The veins on his head and neck were at bursting point. It was then remembered I had a bag of biscuits I had bought in Mbesuma. Maybe that would do the trick? I picked it up, waved it around and said, "Chakula!" (Food!). I then took a great swing and lobbed the packet onto the nearby bank. Like a shot he paddled to the bank and rummaged through it – while I made haste to get away. He didn't follow. If it was like this here in Zambia, what the hell was it going to be like in the Congo?

That night in a moment of delusional romantic foolishness, I wrote the name 'Sting' on my machete with a permanent black marker pen in honour of Bilbo Baggins' sword in *The Hobbit* and *The Lord of the Rings*. I now slept with it every night.

BANGWEULU SWAMP:

Dr Livingstone, I Presume

In Bemba, the word Bangweulu means "where the water meets the sky." Covering an area approximately the size of Derbyshire, Lake Bangweulu and the Bangweulu swamps combined are one of the world's greatest wetland systems. The swamps lie to the south of the lake and in 1991 the area was designated as a wetland of international importance. Seventeen rivers feed the wetlands, the longest being the Chambeshi, but it's drained by only one, the Luapula.

The swamps are completely undeveloped and wild, but many locals still choose to live here, hunting and fishing for survival. At the end of the dry season in July, the southern side of the swamp is almost dry, yet towards the end of the rains in March, the whole of this low-lying area turns into a shallow swamp attracting incredible birdlife and massive amounts of game. As the seasonal cycle progresses, the land begins to dry out again and the animals head back towards the lake.

The famous Dr Livingstone often referred to these wetlands as "a world of water and anthills," since numerous termite mounds are scattered over them. Bangweulu swamp was also where he died, while searching for the source of the Nile in 1873, after succumbing to malaria and internal bleeding caused by dysentery. A not so well known story relating to his death is that of the phenomenal effort of his loyal and trusty attendants, James Chuma and Abdullah Susi, who carried his body one thousand miles back to the east coast. After Livingstone breathed his last, their first act

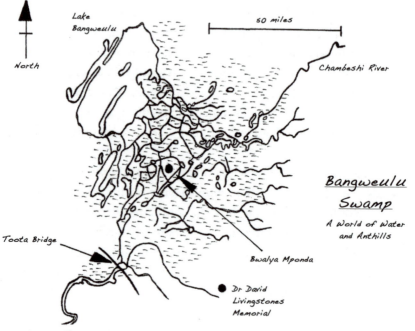

North

Lake
Bangweulu

50 miles

Chambeshi River

Bangweulu
Swamp

A World of Water
and Anthills

Bwalya Mponda

Toota Bridge

Dr David
Livingstones
Memorial

Luapula River

was to remove his internal organs, including his heart, which they buried under a Myula tree in the village of Chipundu (now the site of a Livingstone memorial). They then packed the open trunk of his body with salt as a preservative and dried his corpse under the ferocious African sun. His face was bathed in brandy as an extra preservative and his legs were bent back at the knees to make the final package easier to carry on the epic trek back to the coast – but not before a note was attached to the body. It said: *"You can have his body, but his heart belongs in Africa."* Eleven months after his death his funeral took place at Westminster Abbey in London, where Henry Morton Stanley was one of the coffin bearers.

* * *

A month earlier, back in Lusaka, I had hired the services of a bush pilot by the name of Ed Farmer for a reconnaissance of the swamps, and he had told me there were some pretty big crocodiles in there with a fair share of hippos too. As the maps of the area were so vague, I had wanted to get a bird's eye view to give me a different perspective as to whether I could possibly navigate my way through on my own. The problem with the maps I had was that the level of water was constantly changing, which in turn changed the available channels. I didn't want to end up with nowhere to camp at night in a mosi-infested watery hell, surrounded by hungry crocs.

It was the first time I had ever been in an aeroplane with a propeller on the back, actually pushing the plane along. You could see why Ed loved his job. He would swoop down over the herds of Lechwe (aquatic deer) scattering them in all directions. If he had tried that in England he'd have probably been arrested. He was raving mad and quite a character with a glint in his eye, I liked him immediately. If I hadn't been concentrating so hard on trying not to throw up, I'd have enjoyed more of a laugh with him. I had a pretty good look at the main Chambeshi channel though, and realistically it looked a real challenge to navigate, with multiple interconnecting channels often petering out into thick reed beds.

I had a couple of maps, the best being an A4 size air photograph covering the entire area, and I wanted to get as far as I could on my own before even thinking about hiring a guide. I had previously made sure I knew the local name of the Luapula Bridge ("Toota"), since this was the exit point of the wetlands into the Luapula River, which then formed the trans national border of Zambia and DR Congo.

From the air, it also looked as though there was very little dry land, and as I estimated it would take a week to get through, I also made sure I had enough cold food to eat in the absence of firewood.

I already had a system of sleeping on the water providing the reeds were thick enough. If they were not, my alternative method would be to strap my twenty-litre plastic waterproof food barrel to the side of my canoe acting like an outrigger. Then even if I rolled around in the night, or got hit by something unpleasant, I should stay afloat. Ed told me that most of the human deaths in the area were mostly the result of young children collecting water at night, when the crocs would sneak up on them and pull them under the water, thinking they were animals.

48

As I neared the Bangweulu wetlands I tried to ask for as much information as I could about the names of the few villages there. English was becoming less common and I wanted to make sure if nothing else I could say, "How do I get to so and so village?" in Bemba, along with questions about distance.

I managed to get a fair way in on my own, just by choosing the channel with the main flow, but after a while I had to rely on my compass to pick the right channel – and even then I was getting it wrong. One channel I took got more and more remote, just as darkness fell. I was then forced to machete my way through a thorn-infested thicket, before finding enough dry land to set up camp and some firewood to cook dinner. In the morning, having slept on my canoe, I noticed something a little strange as I looked at the floor. It then dawned on me that it seemed to be moving. Closer inspection revealed it was alive with millions of ants. They were everywhere. Taking down my shelter and packing up camp proved to be rather an unpleasant experience since they were also biting. I ended up chucking everything in the canoe and quickly dragging it through the bush into the water. Then came the tidying and killing phase; first sorting out all my stuff, and then squashing all the little bleeders that had stowed away on board. The ants were not stupid, and when they realised I was a heartless murderer, they scrambled into every nook and cranny to hide; it took weeks to wipe them all out.

★ ★ ★

The turning point came a couple of nights later. My tarp was up so that I could still see all around me, and as my eyes slowly became adjusted to the dark I could just make out the silhouettes of two guys in a dugout canoe right by the bank, and because the bush was quite thick they seemed to be looking for something. When I heard the word Mazungu being mentioned, I started to wonder why they were whispering. Was it out of politeness, so as not to wake me up, or was it because they wanted to slit my throat? I quietly grabbed my machete and put my sandals on, waiting to find out. Maybe if it came to it, the sight of a screaming naked white man brandishing a machete, would be enough to send them running with their tails between their legs. As it turned out they couldn't find a way in – but I didn't get much sleep that night.

So, it was time for a guide, the fount of all knowledge, and, maybe, wise, friendly, sociable... I couldn't wait. From past experience I knew it was often potluck as to whether your guide became the highlight of the trip, becoming a friend and offering great insight into the local village culture, or was a miserable git, who didn't know his arse from his elbow. Having said that, first impressions and gut feelings do count for a lot in my opinion.

"Mulishani, maqui" I said as I passed a guy with his son checking their nets (Bemba for hello and respect).

"Good morning" the man replied. He was called Daniel and turned out to be the best English speaker I had met so far: perfect credentials for a guide.

"Why are you here, I've never seen a tourist in a canoe before?" he said. "Are you not afraid of the crocodiles?"

"I'm here to paddle to the Atlantic Ocean, following the Congo River."

"That's impossible. For a start, you'll never make it through the swamp."

His son was busy untangling a catfish from his net, the friends of which were flapping about in the bottom of their canoe.

"It's funny you should mention that... Actually I'm looking for a guide."

As it turned out Daniel couldn't do it as he had other things on, but he suggested trying at the next village as it was market day and there would be lots of people there. Because he was so helpful and friendly, I gave him one of my T-shirts – his own was in tatters.

"Be careful of the crocodiles, especially at night," he said as I paddled off.

You could tell how often they had tourists in an area by the reaction of the locals. I assumed Bangweulu would have seen its fair share of white folk as it's so famous for its birdlife. The lofty shoebill stork, which feeds on baby crocodiles amongst other things, is one of the biggest lures for twitchers, and is only found both here and in parts of the White Nile in Uganda. As I got further and further into the swamp, with kids running off screaming at the sight of me, bursting into tears and generally with lots of jaw dropping going on, it seemed quite clear that either I looked like some sort of horrific monster, or you didn't get many Mazungus around in the area. I hoped it was the latter.

I didn't really fancy turning up at market day and asking for a guide. When so many people were about, my arrival could turn into a bit of a performance, with me as the centre of attention. You're probably thinking antisocial sod, and to some extent you're probably right, but experience told me market days were events in themselves. It gave the men a chance to let their hair down a bit, while the women did the work of selling their wares. Often the blokes would sit around and get pissed on the local brew, and as had happened before when I turned up, it all gets a bit boisterous. Plus, every man and their dog would see me as a walking bag of cash. This wasn't always the case of course, and often you could make some great friends and have some great experiences, but today I was in the mood for some peace and quiet.

I noticed a tiny fishing village, no more than four huts; I thought it looked good and paddled in. English was pretty rare in these parts, so I had out my Bemba book on deck. This was simply a note pad with various words and phrases I thought might come in handy during conversation. I tried to have it open on deck all the time; that way, if there was no one about I could simply test myself out loud as I was paddling along.

As I came closer, the kids playing by the water froze and stared for a moment, then looked briefly at each other before running to the huts shouting "Mazungu! Mazungu!" The women called the men, and before I had reached the shore, a welcoming committee was making its way down to meet me.

When trying to find a guide, the important thing for me is making sure that whomever you pick knows what you want him to know. Sounds obvious, but it's not as easy as you think. Often the locals want to please you so much that they will tell you anything rather than let you down.

I wanted somebody to guide me to Bwalya Mponda, probably the largest village in the Bangweulu swamp, situated smack bang in the middle of the thing. A sixty-five-years-old man called John said he would be my guide, and told me it would take two to three days to get to Bwayla Mponda, which sounded about right. I asked him if he'd been there before and he frowned and said, "Many times."

My gut reaction was that he was a nice enough bloke – a little bit serious for my liking, his face never cracked a smile, but nice enough. We agreed a price. I told him I'd buy the fish each day if he brought along the nshima; the maize based staple diet of Zambia. Called 'ugali' in East Africa, 'nshima' in Zambia and 'fufu' in Central and West Africa, it's basically what potatoes are to European and American cooking. Depending on what's available locally, it's generally made from yams, cassava or maize, and takes the form of a doughy, starchy accompaniment for stews or whatever is available. To eat, you simply break off a bite sized piece with your right hand, shape it into a ball, making an indentation with your thumb, and use it in place of a spoon to scoop up whatever else you're eating. Cassava, as used in the Congo, is the third largest source of carbohydrates in the world. I'd recommend it; with a nice sauce it's bloody delicious and very filling.

We had to wait for an hour for his wife to get back from the market, so I handed out a few red balloons to the kids which they loved, and demonstrated my flint fire starter to the men. After his wife turned up, he got his things together and put them in my boat. Since his dugout was empty I found this idea a little strange, but he was sixty-five so I let him off. His serious look worried me a little bit, but hey, beggars can't be choosers. We set off at quite a pace, and I think as he kept looking behind he was quite surprised I could keep up.

We arrived at the weekly market and pulled in next to the multitude of dugout canoes. John said he had to buy some nshima. The whole village was probably about half the size of a football pitch, and the huts didn't seem too permanent. Some of them were falling apart, and others seemed to have fallen below the water line. A shabby dog competed with flies to lick a bloody wound on its back, whilst, at the same time, a small naked child played with the creature's tail. Various types of fish were laid out to dry on cotton sheets. The women seemed to be doing all the buying and selling, while I noticed the men sitting in a bit of a circle drinking a white frothy substance. After John bought his nshima, he joined the others in the circle and gave me a look and a nod to join them.

As John sat and drank, the others fired questions at him. He then started to smile for the first time, and I could see he was quite enjoying the attention; some of the women approached him and gave sexy smiles in my direction. He finished his first cup and ordered a youngster to rush off and get him some more. The booze was starting to have an effect on him already. I wondered whether if he drank too much he might not last the day. After his second cup, just as he was asking for a third, I spoke up and reminded him we had a long way to go. When the others realised I could speak some Bemba, they turned their attention on me, and I soon had a cup of the local brew thrust into my hand. Questions came thick and fast – too fast for me to understand a word. Apparently the booze was made from the millions of reeds surrounding us. It tasted terrible and was seriously bitter, but it was clearly very potent and had the desired effect. I managed half a cup and even that made me feel light headed.

The whole time we had been there, I'd had my eye on two shady, very serious looking characters standing in the background, the biggest of whom had a large ugly scar running down his face.

They stared at me constantly and whispered to each other; god knows what. I wondered whether these two were the guys searching for me the other night. Time to go I thought. I clapped my hands together and stood up, John was on his third cup but I insisted he drink up. I said my farewells to the guys, gave a few shekels for the booze and we were off.

John blasted off for about half an hour but soon slowed down to an easy lope. The river was a river no longer. Instead we were surrounded by a myriad of channels, some big, some small. Occasionally it would all open out into large expanses of open water filled with lily pads and beautiful flowers. He certainly knew this area incredibly well, and often took little short cuts right through the reeds, forcing his way through using his pole. Anybody would have thought he was trying to lose me, but with my pole soon assembled I was actually enjoying trying to keep up, quickly having to adapt to the changing environment. The water itself was absolutely crystal clear, not particularly deep, but you could see right to the bottom and I'd often spot fish darting about. All in all it was a beautiful area and untouched by tourism, thank god.

Here, kingfishers were as common as pigeons in Trafalgar square. Big, small, black and white, brightly coloured, they were constantly flying low, skimming over the water. Although Bangweulu's biggest attraction is its birdlife, the endemic black lechwe population is said to be around 100,000 strong, with herds of up to 10,000 antelopes. I didn't see any though. Other animals include sitatunga, reedbuck, oribi, zebra, elephant and buffalo. Hyena, leopard and jackal are occasionally seen although land predators are generally uncommon here.

We passed a tiny fishing camp at one point and five minutes of bartering later we ended up with a three foot catfish which John was ecstatic about. It was his favourite fish. If I had known he had no intention of sharing it, however, or even eating it whilst we were together, I might not have been so generous. (Although, in hindsight, these were selfish thoughts of mine as he planned to take it back to his family. It was buzzing with flies by the time we parted company two days later.)

It later transpired that John had not been entirely honest. Although he had told me he knew the way to Bwayla Mponda, the next morning, after we'd spent a quiet night at a tiny fishing camp, he suddenly seemed very keen to take along another guide. It turned out he hadn't been to Bwayla Mponda for 15 years and had forgotten the way. Not only that, but he still expected me to pay for him and his new guide, a young lad in his late teens named Peter.

We came across Peter at a small floating settlement. The huts had been built on tightly packed bundles of reeds; tall enough to ensure the living area was just above the surface of the water. The trouble was, when I agreed to take him along, his older brother turned up and started smacking him very hard around the head. He basically refused to let him go without his father's permission. Then, after some backchat from Peter, all hell broke loose, with lots of shouting and copious amounts of head slaps. I didn't need this hassle, but in the end we paddled around the corner to find the father, who after a few head slaps of his own, allowed Peter to join us.

Whereas the day before John hardly said a word, this young lad wouldn't stop talking and ended up driving me nuts. He was trying to persuade me to keep him on as a guide to take me all the way to Toota Bridge. He was like a stuck record, repeating the same thing over and over and over again. There was something about him I didn't like, something not quite right, but it wasn't until we reached Bwalya Mponda that I found out what it was.

Bwalya Mponda is the biggest village in the middle of the Bangweulu wetlands and is situated on a small island. The population is about six hundred and it has a school, football pitch and a small medical clinic. On arrival, a lady called Mary – who was secretary to the chief – gave me a tour around the island and took me to see the chief's 'palace', which turned out to be a hut with a tin roof instead of a grass roof. He was away collecting a gift from the Zambian president, who in his infinite wisdom had decided to give selected chiefs around the country a new four-wheel drive vehicle each. This would have been great had his village not been surrounded by a vast expanse of water. Apparently he was trying to exchange it for a motorboat.

The majority of mud brick houses on the island had grass roofs and only a handful had tin roofs. One of these belonged to the assistant chief, whom I was taken to meet. I knew he must be relatively wealthy as there was a large satellite dish on his roof along with a couple of solar panels. The inside was nicer than the place I had been renting in East London prior to the trip, with two plush sofas, armchairs, a carpet, a DVD player, TV and radio. But what really made me laugh was the fact that at the end of our nice little chat, he said to me "but I am so hungry" and looked at me expectantly.

"It's so difficult for me as I don't have money to buy food," he said. But he had enough money to buy all this stuff.

"You cheeky git," I thought.

"You are the assistant Chief and you have this very comfortable house. I think there maybe other people in the village who are in greater need than you," I said.

He got the hint.

I spent two nights on the island. Peter had told everybody he was going to guide me to Toota. After chatting to Mary it transpired he was a drunk and dabbled in other drugs, which explained the red around his eyes and his almost maniacal determination to guide me: more money, more drugs. I had been telling him he was too young, but I then took him to one side and told him I knew the truth, which he, of course, denied.

"Who told you this? You must tell me, who told you this?" he asked angrily, punching his fist into his hand like Batman and Robin.

"Is it true though Peter?" I asked.

He immediately looked at the floor, and almost in tears replied, "No it is not true."

He eventually accepted it, and I gave him some fishing kit as a present.

★ ★ ★

I later found a couple of older guys, Alias and Jonathan who agreed to take me to the bridge. Alias was an old hand with a gammy leg and Jonathan was an all-smiling townie, visiting relatives, who wanted to hitch a lift from Toota to Mansa, a sizeable town. The bartering for the fee took a while as Alias reckoned it would take four days and therefore should be more money. A similar distance however had taken me two days, so I stuck to my guns. He probably thought I wouldn't be able to keep up, not realising I was a paddling machine.

We left next morning and after a short while were poling our way through some pretty difficult waterways. Again they shot off, looking behind to see if I was keeping up, but they soon slowed and assumed a steady pace. Sometimes the grass would be a foot or so high with a tiny passage not deep enough to paddle, and when I tried to stand up and use my pole, it would get stuck in the soft mud and nearly pull me out of my canoe. The locals always stood up to paddle; their heavy hardwood paddles were twice as long as mine and had wide pointed blades. In the soft mud they simply used them as poles, which due to the shape of the blade, never became stuck. After a while I devised a new method, which seemed to work, using the pole like a kayak paddle standing up and pulling it against the grass.

After a few hours of that, the eight-foot high papyrus grass would close in and it would all get pretty close and personal. Poling wasn't an option here as it was too thick with papyrus fronds leaning out into the channel. A samurai sword would have come in handy though. I hit my head many times knocking my baseball cap into the water.

I remembered back to when I had hired Ed Farmer and his bush plane to fly me over Bangweulu.

"It all looks pretty straight forward from up here, but when you are in there you won't have a clue which way to go," Ed had said. He was damn right on that one.

"You do realise you'll probably die," he had also joked. At least I hoped he was joking. I had learned one important lesson in my time: if you listened to everybody who gave you negative advice, you would probably never do anything.

We spent that night on a tiny island no bigger than thirty metres across. There was one grass hut for the two fishermen who lived here, three visiting fishermen and a woman who slept under an improvised tent each. The tents were made from five large rice sacks, which had been sewn together to form a box shape. Four sticks shoved in the ground then supported them. I was told the mosquitoes were apparently bad here. Apart from the hut, the other standard structure was a rack to hold the nets on – and closer inspection revealed the floats were all make from a local type of cork wood; light and extremely buoyant.

Again I felt quite guilty setting up my luxury penthouse dwelling. The lady had a bag full of buns she had made previously, and, seeing this as a valuable opportunity for a buyer, offered them to me for the extortionate price of five pence each. I bought the lot and shared them all around. It made me feel less guilty about my penthouse. Islands like this with firm land were few and far between in these wetlands, and many families resorted to building their own floating huts on reed bundles like Peter's family.

The next afternoon we arrived at the bridge, and Alias wasn't happy with his money (surprise, surprise). I asked him previously how much and how long to take me to the bridge, the price was agreed and he said four days. It took two days as I thought but he still wanted more money. This guy had done a great job, but sometimes they don't. Sometimes they don't even do what they said they would, and then still expect the money and a bonus.

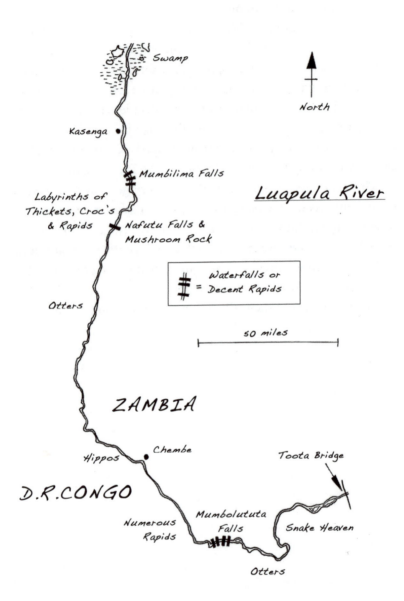

Swamp

North

Kasenga

Mumbilima Falls

Labyrinths of
Thickets, Croc's
& Rapids

Nafutu Falls &
Mushroom Rock

Luapula River

= Waterfalls or
Decent Rapids

Otters

50 miles

ZAMBIA

Chembe

Toota Bridge

Hippos

D.R.CONGO

Numerous
Rapids

Mumbolututa
Falls

Snake Heaven

Otters

THE LUAPULA:

Bandits and Waterfalls

Now that I'd reached Toota Bridge, I'd completed the first major section of my journey. Things were looking good. The next section was the Luapula River, complete with rapids, waterfalls and swamps from here to Nchelege, a village on the banks of Lake Mweru. I estimated it would take ten days. It took twelve.

At the start of this next section, my imagination began freewheeling. In my pre-trip research, I had discovered that this area of river (which formed a trans-national border between Zambia and the Congo) had a bit of a reputation for armed bandits. Apparently they would sneak over from the Congolese side and rob people on the Zambian side before canoeing back across. For this reason I decided to try to remain either undetected in the bush at night, or camp in small villages. The advice I was given in Bangweulu reminded me of the scene in *American Werewolf In London*, when the stars were advised, "Stay off the moor... Keep to the path." Only here it was, "Stay away from the Congo bank... Keep to the Zambian side." I didn't want to let it freak me out, since I would soon have the Congo on both banks. And anyway, it beat watching East Enders.

I came across a fisherman on the first afternoon that seemed quite concerned for my safety; he kept waving me over to the Zambian side, then pointing to the Congo side and shaking his head. It was enough to make anyone paranoid. "It can't be that bleeding bad," I thought.

I found a lovely little camp spot on the Zambian side, and had a nice chat with a one-eyed, hardy looking but friendly fisherman whose hut was a hundred metres along the bank. We were neighbours. Surely he wouldn't sit by and let his neighbour get robbed? Ten minutes later a young girl with a beautiful smile and three kids turned up and asked if I'd like to buy some charcoal, which I did. Then after my standard routine of fire building, food on, dip and wash in the river, change of clothes, mosi-net up and bed made, I sat on the bank and watched an absolutely beautiful sunset. All while tucking into a gourmet meal of chicken kiev and sautéed potatoes. It was actually rice and fish, but you can't blame a man for using his imagination.

* * *

As it turned out, over the next few days, the Congolese bank was totally undeveloped. There were no villages and no human signs, whatsoever. But boy-oh-boy were there a lot of snakes, either on the bank, or swimming in the river. One six-footer actually swam right up to my canoe and reared up a couple of feet out of the water. Another time, in small rapids, as I planted my paddle in the water I noticed something out of the corner of my eye and it was another bloody snake swimming up to the boat. I literally had to fend it off with my paddle.

Otters were another discovery; there were loads of them. Amazing to watch, they would pop up mostly in fast water, and could often be seen swimming under my boat upside down looking at me through the crystal clear water. Occasionally you would also get this bright green weed on the river bottom, which looked like grass blowing in the wind. When it contrasted with the silky brown fur of an otter looking up at me, it was one of those inspirational wildlife moments. One that you don't forget in a hurry. At another point a whole family swam across the river in front of me (otters not people). There little heads staring at me before disappearing below the surface. Some locals told me they were hunted when food was scarce.

Zambia is famous for its abundance of waterfalls, and one of its biggest and most remote was the Mumbolututa waterfall on the Luapula. It was in two stages – and that's about all I knew. I didn't even know when I'd arrive there exactly as I had a pretty basic map, but assumed there would be plenty of fishermen to ask. As it turned out, the day I expected to arrive, there wasn't a soul to be seen, and the water was getting quicker and quicker, and the banks thicker and thicker. Not ideal really. When I'd been canoeing in Canada a couple of years before, there had been a campsite and a landing pontoon at a safe distance above Virginia Falls, with a one-kilometre wooden walkway for portaging the canoe around the falls. This was the complete opposite.

I sensed I was getting close and started to hug the right hand bank. Not long afterwards, I thought I could hear a vague rumbling sound. Unfortunately the right hand bank was virtually impenetrable, with thick ten-foot high grass. I squinted at the river ahead and it didn't look quite right. I couldn't quite make out what was what. I then noticed the spray of the waterfall, and the horizon line before it. The edge couldn't have been more than one hundred and fifty metres away. I had two choices: either to ram myself into the long grass, and somehow claw my way through it onto firm ground, or to paddle like stink and seek refuge in the slack water behind a long thin island in the middle of the river. I chose the island, and before you could say "man eating crocodile" I was tucked nicely behind it, wondering what to do next. At least I had time to think.

I have to admit that some negative thoughts were creeping into my head at this point; namely that maybe I had taken on a bit too much. If it was like this here three weeks in, what would it be like in the DR Congo proper, where there would be even less information about hazards and zero help?

"Stop being such a wimp," I told myself. "You wanted an adventure, well now you've got one. So bloody well get on with it."

I sat there for about twenty minutes weighing up my options – then luckily spotted a couple of fishermen in their dugouts way up stream. I gave them a wave, and they made their way over. If they were coming to me there must be a sneaky way out.

After my best conversation yet in Bemba, they agreed to show me a shortcut to the bank and help carry my boat around the waterfall for a price. We paddled up the side of the island for a bit before ferrying across the river into a tiny wee gap in the grass, which led us through a dark, swampy tunnel of twisting trees and vines before exiting into a more open area. Two rather tiring hours later (with the added help of two other men and later on, a demanding inconvenient third) we made our way back down to the river. Initially the going was pretty tough, and the terrain varied between knee-deep mud, stinking swamp and thick six-foot high grass. But with a combination of half dragging and half paddling, we finally got onto firmer ground and eventually emerged onto a path, which then passed through a small village. The third guy insisted he was the village secretary, and attached himself to us, demanding that I should pay him money for passing through. He was drunk, and stared at me unblinking and wide-eyed. Initially he thought his aggressive attitude would work, but later became all friendly when he realised I wasn't in the mood for his bullshit.

It was dark as we reached the deserted riverbank. After I paid off my incredibly hard working helpers, and persuaded the drunk to leave me in peace, I made camp just below the second, rather impressive set of falls. I was exhausted, bruised and scratched, and as much as I didn't fancy getting in the cold water, or searching around for firewood, I knew a wash and a hot meal would sort me out. The water was freezing and firewood was hard to find in the dark, but I felt much better as I sat under my mosi net, fully refreshed, and started tucking into some hot grub.

People often moan about sleeping out in the tropics, dark at six and light at six with twelve hours to kill under your mosi-net. But for me, after nine or ten hours paddling a day it was bliss; twelve hours of recuperation after a hot meal. I honestly don't think I would have made it had I not had this rest.

★ ★ ★

For some reason I had assumed the river would be calm after the falls, since there was no mention of rapids on the map. But I was in for a bit of a surprise the next morning. Apart from waking up to find two guys just standing over me staring, I was surprised to discover the rapids were not finished.

The thing about paddling rapids on your own, especially in a wilderness environment, is that you'd have to be a raving mad man to paddle them blind. In other words, not having a clue what's ahead, but paddling on anyway. If they are easy and you can see everything in front of you, fair enough. If not, you could get sucked into something nasty, with no time to get out. Adrenaline inducing yes, but not very sensible if you don't want to end up as fish food. The safer option when in doubt is to get out and scout ahead. My more dominant adventurous side loved paddling the rapids, but the faint voice of Mr. Sensible craved calmer waters. The rapids lasted for the rest of the day.

I paddled them all, but had to get out and walk along the bank on occasion to check what was around the next corner. There wasn't a dwelling or fisherman to be seen; only a few snakes and horrible looking spiders. Unfortunately the latter's webs were often right on the water's edge. Given the choice I'd much prefer drowning to a mass arachnid attack.

The hills loomed either side and when they finally flattened out and the river became calm again. I paddled over to the first fisherman I had seen since my morning stalkers and asked if the rapids had finished. When he said it's flat until the distant village of Chembe I could have kissed him – but gave him a packet of cigarettes instead. I sang out loud as I paddled off, chuffed to bits my confidence hadn't taken a knock.

★ ★ ★

Chembe was the first named village of significance on the river so far, and I had imagined all sorts of tempting luxuries would be on offer there. The Chinese were building a bridge, creating an important trade shortcut to Lubumbashi, and the difference on either side was stark. The Zambian side had a brick police and immigration building, a tarmac road with a large metal gate and lots of people in uniform. The Congolese side had a gaggle of people, a dirt track and a few straw huts… and that was it. Luckily for me I was greeted by the chief of police, who, more importantly, was friendly.

While he quizzed me, I couldn't help my attention being drawn to some ladies selling fried fish on the side of the road, damn they smelt good. Old trucks whose springs were held together with strips of rubber, with tires that probably failed their M.O.T back in the sixties, were jam packed with people having just crossed over on the rather rundown looking ferry. My letter from the Zambian Tourist Commission did the trick again, and before I could say "ere darling sell us your fried fish," a Land Cruiser had been summoned to take my canoe and me to the best guesthouse in town. Not before I bought enough fried fish to feed a small army though.

The guesthouse was luxury. I had my own room, a double mattress on the floor, a candle and a well out the back with a bucket on a rope for washing. It beat sleeping in a swamp. The one restaurant in town had run out of food, so the fried fish, some bananas and groundnuts (peanuts) did the trick.

As I had drawn so much attention on arriving, I thought I'd leave at dawn the next day before any unsavoury characters were up and about. The policeman in charge of the ferry picked me up at six, and told me there was still fighting going on in the border town of Pweto. This was the border town where I would enter DR Congo from Zambia on Lake Mweru.

I need not have worried about drawing much attention to myself, as there was a heavy thick mist on the river with visibility down to a few metres. I was, however, warned that I should wait until it cleared as there were a few hippos just downstream, and the last thing I wanted to do was surprise one. I waited for about half an hour, but it still wasn't clearing so I set off anyway. Although I heard the distinctive grunts of hippos nearby, the only thing I nearly hit was the half finished bridge.

The next major obstacle according to the map was Mumbilima Falls, a four-mile long stretch of small waterfalls quite close to a major road. I was more than a little surprised then to discover something else that wasn't on the map. A couple of days before Mumbilima, the river was a couple of hundred metres wide, all very easy and straightforward.

Then, all of a sudden, a wall of jungle confronted me and the river disappeared into it in a myriad of channels, with no suggestion as to what was the best route, or how long it would last. It was potluck.

I'd known these labyrinths existed but hadn't expected them here. The danger was – as I was soon to discover – that the gradient would often drop away ending with rapids or even waterfalls, and if you went the wrong way you might get sucked in before you could do anything about it. Alternatively there might only be easy rapids in there and after ten minutes you'd be back on the open river again. The hardest thing was not knowing. It could take you a whole day to get through going the wrong way, fighting your way back upstream, jumping out into waist deep water and dragging the canoe – or it could be a piece of cake.

The first one was indeed a piece of cake, the second one I had directions from a fisherman who waved for me to go to the right hand side, a little longer with a few rapids but not too bad. The third one in the same day was a little more difficult. I turned back a couple of times as I didn't like the look of things, and I heard a distant roar of white water. I then bumped into another fisherman who said he'd show me part of the way in, but after that I'd have to carry the boat around, as it was too dangerous.

Whenever I followed a dugout it took a lot of worry off my mind. Thumb up bum, mind in neutral. I could relax and enjoy the wilderness environment. Fish would jump, eagles would swoop and sometimes an otter would pop up for a look. My canoe was a lot more capable of handling harder white water than their dugouts, so I knew I could easily handle whatever they were prepared to paddle.

After some easy rapids and a lovely windy route through some dense forest with laser beams of sunlight piercing the canopy, my guide stopped at his hut and explained I would have to carry my canoe around from there. I jumped out and walked down the bank for a while, and sure enough there was larger rapid with a few rocks in the middle, but I was quite confident I could paddle it with no dramas. He shook his head and said a bit further down it got a lot worse. Finally he agreed to walk down to where it gets worse, and point it out to me, so I paddled the first bit, then sure enough further down there was something more substantial.

It even had a name: Nafutu falls. I'd never heard of it, and it certainly wasn't on the map. It wasn't a waterfall, but it was a decent rapid, and the forest had abruptly disappeared, giving way to a small gorge with a unique mushroom shaped rock at the bottom where the water had eroded it for thousands of years. I walked down to inspect it, and it actually looked quite paddle-able, albeit very boily. Basically the whole river was squeezed into a passage of about thirty feet wide. Boils are formed when a lot of water is forced through a disproportionately small gap, creating surging, rotating areas of water. When they're powerful, they can be extremely hard to paddle through and stay upright.

I asked the guy on the bank to come down and help pick up the pieces should I capsize, but all he could do was shake his head with a worried look on his face. It was a beautiful day and I was enjoying myself, I knew I could do it. I was far from anywhere and on my own and I knew it wasn't particularly sensible, but carrying the canoe around would have taken a lot of time and effort – and besides, I needed my adrenalin fix.

As soon as I paddled into the current, and felt the power of the water I knew I couldn't afford to screw up. It was at times like this when I felt most alive, absolutely present in that moment, with nothing cluttering the mind other than the total concentration needed to do the job. This was a time for positive thoughts only. I knew I was perfectly capable of paddling the rapid. I had the experience. But I also knew that one mistake could lead to heartache. What I didn't have much experience of was the power of the boils, and just before the end I got slightly off line... and that was enough. Before I could do much about it, a surging rotating boil spun me around like a cork. I found myself paddling backwards, which wasn't particularly pleasant. I managed to stay afloat though.

Just as I thought I'd had my excitement for one day, after an hour of open river I was confronted by another wall of jungle. It was weird because I started the day surrounded by grass covered hills, then into a jungle labyrinth followed by a rocky gorge, and now I was facing a wall of gnarled and twisted vines and thick greenery. The river of two hundred metres wide had once again dissolved into twenty smaller channels disappearing under the canopy.

As I was feeling quite confident, I thought, bugger it, I'll stick to the left hand side and go it alone. In I went, and it felt like a different world. The vegetation hadn't been this thick before. I could hear a permanent rumbling of rapids somewhere off in the distance, and tried to keep to the left hand side, not wanting to lose my bearings in the middle. Every now and then the rapids would increase so I'd try to backtrack and find the easiest path. I ducked under one vine only to disturb a crocodile slithering off a rock. The canopy at this point was all enveloping, with hardly any visible sky. As uncertain as I was, this was definitely what it was all about, and not having a bloody clue about what lay ahead, made the experience all the more adventurous. At times the current was fast, requiring quick decision-making, and a constant need to read the surface of the water, to choose the best route, along with a need to look ahead to make sure I didn't get sucked into a tangled thicket. Then, all of a sudden, the flow seemed to stop, and I'd find myself paddling upstream without realising it, all the while hearing the distant rumble of rapids god knows where. Sometimes I'd spot a better channel through the greenery and have to squeeze my way through the tiniest of gaps, taking great care not to cut myself to pieces on the most horrendous thorny vines I'd ever seen.

But it really was a unique environment and although very harsh, it was quite beautiful. Part of me didn't want to leave, but after a couple of hours I turned back as the rapids were getting too big with no room to scout. There must be a safer way through.

When I finally emerged back out into the sunlight where I had started, I met Chalwe, a Congolese fisherman, slightly built and very serious who only spoke Swahili. He told me nobody ever goes through to the other side, as the rapids were too big, and there were too many crocodiles. I explained what I was doing and that I sometimes pay for a guide and he agreed to try to take me through.

But after another hour of exploring and backtracking, having a close encounter with a particularly large croc, we returned to the beginning and he refused payment. He suggested we try again the next day.

I then met Ivor and his dad George, out checking their nets. George was sixty-nine and had eleven children. His smile was infectious. Ivor spoke good English and asked if I'd spend the night at there camp, which was a small clearing amongst six foot high grass, with a log fire in the middle. No shelter or beds of any kind. Ivor and his dad were real characters, and epitomised the sort of locals I loved to meet. Always laughing and mischievous, confident yet respectful, and they never once asked me for a thing. Only towards the end of the evening did Ivor tell me about the farm he was trying to build for his family, and asked if I knew anyone who had any old farming equipment for sale. His dad had obviously brought him up to be a proud moral guy and I was quite humbled by their quality as human beings.

I cooked enough rice for us all, shared out my kapenta and we sat around the fire for a couple of hours chatting. America seemed to be their Holy Grail, and Ivor didn't stop asking questions about it, busily translating back to the others. As a mangy dog warmed itself by the fire, I told them how in America there are whole shops devoted to selling luxuries for pets. That these sold jackets, booties, even diamond jewellery, and that some women carried their dogs everywhere they went. They were in hysterics, and continued sniggering for ages as they curled up on the floor around the fire.

The next morning Chalwe returned with his mate Kivu, who apparently knew a way through. The problem was that due to the rapids and falls, they wouldn't be able to return with their canoe until the next rainy season in a few months time, so would have to charge more money. Ivor confirmed this was true so we negotiated a price and set off. I wished Ivor all the best with his farm.

★ ★ ★

For four hours we manhandled our boats through all manner of natural obstacles. At times we were dragging our canoes upstream up to our chests in the water, and sometimes we had to create our own shortcuts by machete-ing our way through hanging liana vines. Having a long piece of floating rope attached to either end of my canoe helped enormously, as on some rapids with too many rocks all I had to do was carefully push it out into the current and use the ropes to gently lower it down under control, without risk to myself. The dugout, however, would often require all three of us to jump into the water and manhandle it down under control. Eventually we emerged at the bottom only to be told at the next village that the Mumbilima Falls were just around the corner.

Those four hours were what I would call a real adventure, and they told me no white man had ever gone through there before. I was more determined now than ever to make it to the Atlantic.

Even so, Mumbilima Falls was not really an option. Part of me wanted to attempt it, but everybody had said it would be suicide, that I'd be sucked into a waterfall and that that would be it. At this point there was a road on the Zambian side of the river, the first since Toota Bridge, so I recruited some help to carry my canoe to the road and waited two hours for a lift. The falls were only a couple miles long and before I knew it I was back on the river below the falls. From what I could see from the road, there were a lot of small waterfalls with many islands and trees in between. Maybe I should have attempted it, but it was too late now. Patrick, who gave me the lift, spoke good English and helped me carry my canoe to the river from the village on the road. He told me how he was studying to be a doctor, and already performed operations at the local clinic after two years training. He was the only person in town who owned a car.

Back on the river, I estimated three days to get to Nchelenge, the last town on the eastern shore of Lake Mweru and my destination on this leg. In the end it took me four. I was now in the middle of the Luapula swamps, surrounded on all sides by eight-foot high papyrus grass. The main river remained wide and clear all the way to the lake, but the trouble was that it started to meander wildly, with relentless headwinds. At one point, even paddling as hard as I could, I was being blown back upstream. When it was like this, it didn't take long to run out of energy. Canadian canoes are great, but not for paddling into a headwind for days on end. Enough was enough.

I decided to take a shortcut through the swamps to Mofwe Lagoon, and then back into the swamps again before hopefully coming out somewhere near Nchelenge. Following a compass bearing of north-east I set off through a tiny channel into the swamp, and within minutes became enveloped in a tunnel of papyrus grass. The sunlight was almost blocked out, but, more importantly, so was the wind. The swamp was interlaced with interconnecting passageways, either made by fishermen with machete cuts, or where something had forced its way through, flattening all before it. The whole area looked like a crocodile and hippo heaven, and every now and then I'd come across a small lagoon with beautiful flowers and giant lily pads on the surface, with god knows what lurking beneath. The tunnels were sometimes too narrow to paddle, and too overhanging to stand up and use a pole. All I could really do was push off the sides, trying not to get a slap in the face from the elastic like papyrus. It became a tad tiring after a while. Again I felt like Humphrey Bogart in the film *The African Queen*. If it hadn't been for mosquitoes the size of dragonflies feasting on my A-positive, and blowing dog whistles in my ears, I'd have been having a ball. When I finally emerged out into Lake Mweru, a rather bemused looking fisherman told me I was the first white man he had ever known to cross through the swamps. I'd heard that one before.

★ ★ ★

Five miles distant as the crow flies was the town of Nchelenge. I could either hug the coast, which would be longer, or go for the open crossing. As the wind usually dropped in the evening, I went for the latter. The last hour was in the dark, but a distant light and the thought of a bed and fried chicken spurred me on. The light turned out to be a heavily guarded and fenced off port owned by a foreign mining company, with its own power supply. They were a bit surprised when I turned up.

"You cannot stay here, you must leave, this is private property," said the night watchman.

"This is the only light in Nchelenge. Would you rather I take my chances with the crocodiles? You know they hunt at night?"

"I must phone the manager."

I don't think he wanted a dead Mazungu on his conscience.

The manager arrived in his jeep ten minutes later and agreed to store my canoe for the night. He then very kindly offered to drive me to a guesthouse in town. The streets were black as a result of the nightly power cuts, and the only lights came from tiny homemade oil lamps on various stalls lining the main street. I stuffed my face with two plates of sausage and chips and four cokes at the guesthouse. When the power came back on I was shocked at my reflection in the mirror. After just over a month on the river, my hands were blistered and bloody from a twelve-hour paddling day, my nose and cheeks were burnt to a crisp and I was the proud owner of the best six-pack I'd had in years.

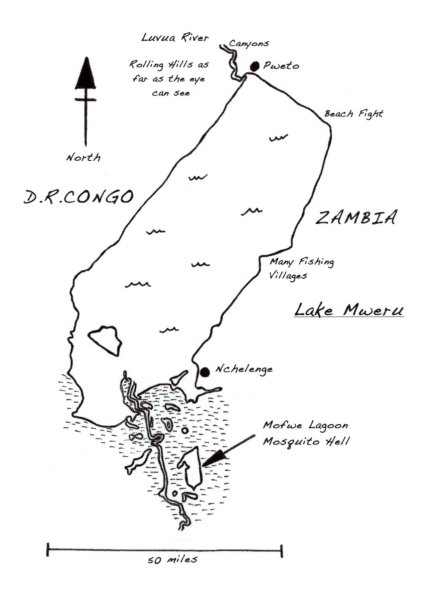

Luvua River   Canyons

Rolling Hills as
far as the eye
can see

North

D.R.CONGO

Pweto

Beach Fight

ZAMBIA

Many Fishing
Villages

Lake Mweru

Nchelenge

Mofwe Lagoon
Mosquito Hell

50 miles

LAKE MWERU

Tanks and White Caps

Lake Mweru is about seventy miles long and thirty miles wide; practically an inland sea. At night it's lit up with fishing boats, oil lamps blazing. In the early morning the netting boats paddle out furiously, dragging the nets off the beach and forming a giant circle before paddling back in hoping to land a bumper catch. The men then haul the net in, carefully pulling up the last section, which is more of a fine mesh. The catch I witnessed was a couple of buckets full of tiny fish no bigger than your little finger, enough to feed four or five families for the day.

In Nchelenge I spent a few days resting, eating and practicing my Swahili. This was the last town in Zambia before the border. After the lake it would be into DR Congo, and Bemba no more. As there was no Zambian immigration at the lake border I got my exit stamp in Nchelenge, and phoned Mr. Zulu back in Lusaka at the same time. Technically I was in no-man's land for the four days it took to paddle to the border.

The wind was both a blessing and a curse. I'd be up and on the water by six am. By eight, the wind picked up from behind, up would go my improvised sail of a giant rice sack on my two wooden poles and I'd be off. I could lie back, put my feet up and steer with my paddle, bliss! Steadily the wind would get stronger until waves started breaking into the canoe, then the wind would start to change direction, down would come the sail, and it was up to paddle power to stop myself getting blown onto the shore. Because of the steep hills bordering the lake, to get the best wind it was necessary to paddle at least a mile off shore. After a couple of hours of paddling, my strength would give out and I'd eventually get blown ashore in the early afternoon; exhausted and often greeted by a whole village.

It was very tempting to paddle further out where the wind was stronger. On one occasion I was probably a couple of miles out surfing the waves, when I was overtaken by a cheering group of fishermen in their rather impressive fishing boat. It was probably twice the length of my canoe, with brightly coloured plank sides. The guy at the back steered with his paddle in the absence of a rudder, but what really stood out was the massive 'square rig' sail, which looked like something off of a pirate ship. The mast was completely home made from a couple of pieces of bamboo, while the sail itself was made from about fifteen rice sacks split open and hand sewn together.

On the right hand side of the lake you had Zambia, with DR Congo on the left hand side, and the wind often dictated where you spent a lot of your time. If they were out at night and the wind changed direction, these fishermen might be away from their families for a week or more. Then with a constant strong onshore wind blowing onto their own shoreline, they might not even be able to get off the beach to fish at all.

The day before the border I thought I'd cut off the corner of the lake, which meant paddling a few miles offshore. The weather was so warm, I thought that if I capsized, as long as I kept hold of the canoe I'd be okay – if I couldn't manage that, a three mile swim wasn't the end of the world. I hadn't seen any crocs about.

By early afternoon I was surrounded by white-capped waves, and they were starting to break into the canoe, filling it up. It was as rough as I'd ever paddled in, but in the far distance I spotted a long white beach and decided to head for that. In rough water, the last thing you want to be is rigid, and as I surfed the waves I fell into a sort of meditative, trance like state, totally relaxed. I was in the zone and it felt great.

The distant beach was lined with straw huts as far as the eye could see, there were some fishing boats pulled up on the sand but I was homing in on a large tree offering some welcome shade. As I drew closer I noticed the odd pig, then a groups of ducks waddling along the waters edge. I love pigs, and as these ones watched me floating past I was reminded me of a quote by Sir Winston Churchill: "I like pigs. Dogs look up to us. Cats look down on us. Pigs treat us as equals."

I surfed onto the beach, I quickly jumped out and dragged the canoe up as far as I could. Two young guys came running down to help. But when they got close and realised I was white, they turned and ran off. I called out hello and explained myself in Bemba, and hesitantly they returned and helped me drag the canoe into the shade of the tree. Within fifteen minutes there must have been sixty people crowded around to see what all the fuss was about. Luckily one guy, Peter, spoke excellent English, and translated to the rest, explaining who I was and where I had come from. The older men gathered around the canoe, and were confused as to where the engine was, then shook their heads in disbelief when I told them I only had a paddle. I loved it when they realised I was a fellow canoeist, because it meant we shared a common bond, and went a long way to breaking down barriers between us. I just wished I understood the language better.

So keen were the crowd to help me unpack that it all turned a bit nasty. Two men tried to help me untie some rubber straps, both trying it a different way, and I corrected one of them. The other guy then said something, which must have been along the lines of, "Ha ha you got it wrong, you nugget", because next minute they both stood up and laid into one another with their fists, and grappled each other to the floor. These guys were built like brick shit houses, and there were some serious blows to the head. The women started cheering, the old men shaking their heads and some other guys tried to drag them apart. All I wanted to do was get a fire going and get my rice on the go.

After a while the others tried to make them shake hands, but then something was said and it all kicked off again, this time they fell over my canoe, knocking me over as well. Eventually it all calmed down, and people started wandering off until I was left with a permanent fan club of about fifteen youngsters just sitting and staring at everything I did. In the end, I went up and sat right next to them and stared at the canoe, occasionally pointing at it and laughing. They were soon in hysterics. The same thing happened in virtually every village (not the fight), where the locals would intently study me making a fire, cooking, eating, washing up, bathing, cleaning my teeth and even going to the toilet. I got used to it all, apart from when I went for number two. I had my limits. If an alien landed on this planet, I'd be interested, but not enough to want to observe his bowel movements.

Peter said it would be fine to camp under the tree for the night, and within seconds of lying down I was fast asleep. I was awoken in the middle of the night by the unmistakable sound of someone cocking an automatic rifle – or at least that's what it sounded like. I sat bolt upright and grabbed my machete, straining all my senses for any information as to what was lurking in the pitch-blackness. Sure enough, another weapon was cocked and I heard footsteps closing in.

"Get up," somebody close shouted.

I needed to get off on the right foot.

TOP LEFT: *Precarious crossing of Log bridge in Zaire, one slip and we were off*
ABOVE: *Pat digging us out of the mud, he had Typhoid at the time*
LEFT: *Shooting the rapids on the South Nahanni River, Canada, in preparation for the Congo*
BELOW: *Jubilant screaming kids in north east Zambia*

ABOVE: *Catch of the day in a beautifully made fish-trap*
BELOW: *Struggling to navigate through Bangweulu Swamp*

ABOVE: *Bemba woman and her child in the crocodile infested Chambeshi flats*
BELOW: *My one-eyed neighbour, first night on the Luapula*

ABOVE: *Ivors father George Mamby*

ABOVE: *Beautiful girl who sold me charcoal*
LEFT: *Yellow toothed gentleman warning me of bandits*

RIGHT: *Four
dead Coypu
hunted with
spears and dogs*
MIDDLE:
*Poling my way
through
Bangweulu
Swamp*
BELOW:
*Mumbolotuta
falls on the
Luapula River*

ABOVE: *Giving the kiss of life to a local delicacy*

ABOVE: *Rapids worthy of a short portage on the middle Luvua river*
LEFT: *Heavily armed local in the hills surrounding Pweto*

LEFT: *Dugout 'carpark' in the shade*
BELOW: *Unique haircuts on Bamu Island, Malebo Pool*
BOTTOM: *Being guided around some nasty rapids*

ABOVE: *Grass covered hills surrounding 'the gates of hell',*
being burnt down for farming
BELOW: *Three very happy kids with homemade toy in Lokuleyla*

ABOVE: *Waterfall fisherman with simple scoop net*
BELOW: *One of three perfectly intact, rusted solid steam engines in Kongolo*

TOP: *One of many
rusting decaying
riverboats littering the
shore at Kongolo*
BELOW & LEFT:
*Various abandoned
rivercraft, including
the remnants of an
old paddle steamer*

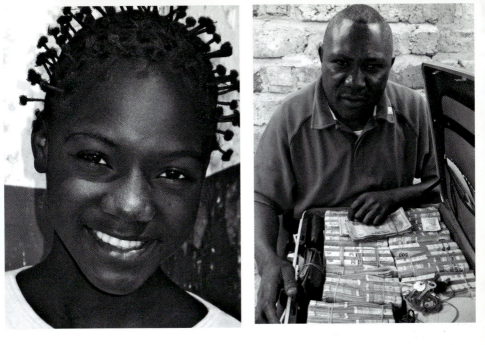

ABOVE: *The prettiest girl in Kisangani and a not so pretty money changer*
BELOW: *Kongolo's all smiling station master. There was one train a month*

ABOVE: *Wagenia fisherman and some racks of dried fish for sale*
RIGHT: *Enormous scoop net requiring tremendous skill and balance to use*
BELOW: *Janvier … a fine travelling companion on the lower Congo River*

TOP RIGHT: *Dodging trees carrying my canoe through the jungle around some falls*
BELOW: *Wagenia fisherman at Stanley Falls (Lots of small fish = One big fish)*

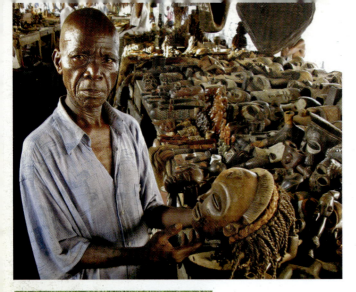

LEFT: *Mask salesman in the capital, Kinshasa*
RIGHT: *Maurice(left), Valatay, Leonardo and John having a wash just before we arrived in Mbandanka*

LEFT: *Lone Hippo wary of hunters below the 'bush meat' capital of Mbandanka*
BELOW: *A serious fishing spear demonstrated in the village of Lokuleyla*
RIGHT: *Paddling machines Leonardo, John and Valatay*

ABOVE: *Situated in the mangrove swamps close to the Angolan border. This was the chief of 'mussel shell' village on hearing I was going to give him my canoe as a gift*

RIGHT: *Collecting, boiling and skewering mussel and clam meat was all part of the daily life for these fine people I met on the last night of my journey*

BELOW: *The back streets of Kinshasa*

"Get up please!" I returned defiantly.

"Who are you?" coming again out of the darkness.

"Who are you?" I replied, pushing my luck maybe with the verbal ping pong match.

"We are the Zambian police, show us your papers," came a voice closely followed by a torch shining in my face. There were six of them, and after I showed them my passport and letter from the tourist board, and I explained what I was doing here and they seemed to relax. Satisfied I wasn't up to no good, they eventually left – at which point Peter turned up and told me they had thought I was a mercenary.

The next day was the windiest yet. By seven o'clock in the morning it was blowing a hooley, and directly onto the shore. Even the local boats were not going out, but I was determined to cross the border. After being blown ashore at one village, meeting the chief, and having a brief rest, the whole village gathered to watch me paddle out through the surf, cheering every time I ploughed through a wave. They reckoned I wouldn't make it, and it was touch and go at one point, but after I got out past the breakers, even though the canoe was half full of water it got a lot easier. Finally I noticed a red flag on a pole in the reeds and realised it must be the border.

★ ★ ★

The policeman back at Chembe on the Luapula had told me there was still fighting in Pweto, and as a result, there was a large military presence there. Pweto was situated right in the north west corner of the lake where the Luvua River exited. At approximately 200 miles long, this river was one of the most remote stretches of the entire trip and in my research I could find no information on it at all. One map I found showed three sets of waterfalls but little else. Pweto seemed like a fitting gateway to nowhere The dilapidated, half beached houseboat I saw when I arrived gave an indication as to the state of the place. A family seemed to have made it their home despite the large holes in the hull and the constant buffeting of the waves. As I loomed out of the stormy waters my pale skin soon had heads double taking, and within seconds the word Mazungu was being screamed from all directions.

I hadn't even stopped surfing up onto the beach before enthusiastic hands dragged my canoe further up with me still in it. Some were children but most were partially uniformed soldiers eager to take me to their leader, who turned out to be the head of the Katanga province "Force Navale", or so he claimed. Of course first there was the matter of paying the fifteen people who absolutely insisted on carrying my boat fifty metres up the beach. Deep down, I probably am a bit of a soft touch, but I'm no mug, and if there's one thing that winds me up, it's people trying to boss me about. I told them I wouldn't pay anything as I could drag the canoe myself, but they wouldn't listen, and gathered around all wanting their cut. I waved my hands up and down to get some quiet to speak and they finally got the hint. I had my platform and in my best French said: "Thank you for your help, I will give you a cigarette if you want," and held out a packet.

"Give us money," some of them shouted.

"It's your choice," I said, shrugging my shoulders, putting the cigarettes in my pocket, turning and walking off to the boss's hut.

A couple of the more aggressive ones grabbed my arm, which I wasn't particularly happy about. I knocked their arms away, going eyeball to eyeball with the nearest and said, "Pas toucher moi monsieur, vous comprenez?"

It seemed to do the trick.

Luckily I seemed to hit it off with the head guy, Xavier. He was chilled and spoke a little bit of English. It turned out when their borders consisted of lakes and rivers; the Government had posted naval personnel to the area. They had no boats but probably a hundred personnel, not including the army and police. Xavier had also spent time with the American navy in the Pacific, and seemed quite keen for me to watch the morning parade, giving me a chair overlooking the proceedings.

It was a spectacular setting. To the right stood grass covered hills turned golden with the early morning sun, and to the front the vast expanse of Lake Mweru, peppered with white-capped waves.

"Informal" could be the best word to describe the parade, and considering the guys hadn't been paid in six months, who could blame them? As one sergeant lined everybody up for inspection, another staggered around drunk as a lord. A couple of the rank and file started arguing, and when the sergeant intervened they started on him. One shout from the boss alongside me however, and it all calmed down. The ten or so soldiers lining up probably had about four complete uniforms between them, and some of them were barefoot. As easy as it is to criticise, I'm sure they had a fair amount of combat experience, and at the end of the day, that's a lot more important than shiny boots. I thought back to when I did drill, and, the sadistic lunatic of a drill sergeant who would make you run at full speed and jump off of a bench into a six-foot hedge if your thumb wasn't exactly in line with the seam of your trousers.

★ ★ ★

I ended up stashing my canoe in the local armoury, the only building around with a chain and padlock. I had to clamber over rusting AK47's, rocket launchers and mortar rounds all covered in a thick layer of dust, to squeeze it in.

Usually the words "Congolese Immigration Officials" and "trustworthy" don't really go together, but in Pweto, things were a little different. It took me 10 days, and a lot of worry to realise this, however. Basically they couldn't extend my two-week visa because they didn't have the required stamp. I needed a three to six month visa.

The older I get, the more I believe in trusting your gut feeling. And when I spent the afternoon chatting to the three immigration

83

guys, I believed they were telling the truth, especially John. His head was as round as a ball, he always wore a light blue tracksuit, he spoke five languages and every expression he ever mustered was delivered almost exclusively through his eyes. The bottom line was they didn't have a stamp, and even if they did have one, they didn't have the authority to give a longer visa. The only option was therefore to get one in Lubumbashi, a three day four-wheel-drive ride away – or two days on the back of a trial bike. Another possibility – and the one I ended up going with – was to fly my passport there and back on the Aid Agency light aircraft that supposedly flew in and out two to three times a week. I tried to fly myself but nobody would take me.

My passport flew out the day after I arrived and so they said, got stamped the same day. Then began a torturous, debilitating ten-day waiting game. There were no flights back for a week, and when a flight finally arrived, guess what wasn't on it? I was then informed the head of immigration in Lubumbashi wanted me to fly there and meet him face to face, and he wouldn't take no for an answer. Apparently he thought I was going to die on the river, and wanted to make sure I could look after myself. But as much as I tried, none of the aid agencies or mining companies would take me, as I wasn't insured. Upon seeing a UN Chinook helicopter coming in to land one day, I waved down the first motorbike that passed and flashed some dollars for him to take me to where it was landing. It was unloading barrels of diesel, and was due to fly back to Lubumbashi empty, but as much as I begged the Dutch pilot to take me (showing him my Winston Churchill Fellowship letter), the rulebook said no passengers to be taken when fuel is or has been carried. What a load of rubbish. I'd travelled in enough helicopters to know otherwise, all you had to do was open the bloody window. The Western world is full of jobsworths, and that for me is partly why Africa appealed so much. One of my favourite sayings is: "Rules are for the blind obedience of fools, and for the guidance of wise men."

Apparently a year before Pweto had been in the hands of the Mai Mai Rebels. This explained why I had come across so many abandoned tanks in the surrounding hills. One of these, a Russian T62, was left overlooking the town, almost perfectly intact. Like a big kid I couldn't resist hanging off the barrel and swinging it around, only to jump off and find myself coming face to face with a scary looking guy and an equally scary looking home made dagger on his belt. He was also brandishing an ancient looking AK47 assault rifle, which he gripped to his chest like a newborn child. It turned out he was probably more scared of me than I was of him, thank God, and I ended up giving him some cigarettes in return for taking a picture.

Pweto was quite a bustling little town, fortunately situated right on the border with Zambia, and with the road access bringing in much needed goods. It pretty much consisted of one long dirt road, running from the top of a gentle hill all the way down to the lake. There was a covered fish and vegetable market where most of the action took place, a few stores, and a smaller side alley selling second hand clothes. Lining the street were various people sitting on crates with makeshift tables. There was fresh tea and bread for sale, groundnuts, cigarettes, rubber sandals made from car tyres and a selection of cheap electrical goods. One section had a row of singer sewing machines, with young girls busy at work.

From Pweto you only really had a dirt track, a terrible journey by all accounts, accessible by four-wheel-drive to Lubumbashi, and that's it. Other than that, there are footpaths heading off into the hills, and the Luvua River which is dotted with waterfalls and rapids and surrounded by hundreds of miles of wilderness.

I had thought about buying a handgun for protection on this trip, and I reckoned now would be my best chance. AK47's were ten a penny and widely available but a tad conspicuous for my liking, not exactly something you could hide down your trousers. A handgun would be perfect. Only the higher-ranking soldiers seemed to carry holsters on their belts. I approached one guy on the street whom, much to my amazement, and to his embarrassment revealed that his sidearm was actually a plastic toy.

I put the word out that I was looking for a gun via my mate Jason who ran the guesthouse in which I was staying. I met an army major that afternoon in the street, who said he could help me. He was in full uniform with armed underlings following him around like baby ducklings, but he didn't seem such a bad sort. We arranged to go to his house one night shortly afterwards. Jason came along and – after winding our way by torchlight through a warren of mud huts – we arrived. After pushing through a blanket which hung in place of a door, we were invited in and sat at a table lit by an ageing oil lamp. He put the gun on the table and I immediately recognised it as a British Browning 9mm, which, as it turned out, was still loaded. Shoot 'em both, free gun, I immediately thought. As if reading my mind the guy asked for it back and unloaded it. He wanted $200, but as I stripped it down I discovered the firing pin was rusted solid. NO SALE. I offered to try to fix it the next day, but he assured me he could do it, and that was the last I heard of him. A few days later somebody else offered me another, and although it was a nice little gun he wouldn't drop below $700. I don't think so. My trusty machete would have to do.

★ ★ ★

As telephone landlines don't exist in DR Congo, and due to the unreliability of the mobile phone coverage, I had allowed the immigration guys to phone Lubumbashi with my sat-phone on occasion. Though they wouldn't allow me to speak to anyone myself, I had the number on my phone.

After a week of promises and let downs regarding flights, and after I had tried to re-enter Zambia without a passport, in order to hitch around to nearer Lubumbashi, and been forcibly escorted back by soldiers, I realised I would have to think of something fast.

The deserted dirt airstrip was on top of a hill overlooking the village. Whilst waiting for a flight one day, I met my first Englishman working for a mining company, who I grabbed and shook by the shoulders so pleased was I to meet him. He looked a bit silly though, like he had been to Harrods and asked to be kitted out in the latest safari outfit. Everything Khaki coloured. Shorts, shirt, big leather belt, white socks rolled up over the top of his desert boots; he even had a ridiculous Indiana Jones hat. He then told me he had had his passport and four thousand dollars stolen by the immigration officer in the immigration office in Lubumbashi. And as the immigration officer was a mate with the police chief, nothing was done. Bastards!

The immigration guys and a tough looking soldier had driven me up to the airstrip. When the English bloke finally gave up waiting, he left with his driver and I was suddenly left all alone, as my guys had walked off along the airstrip chatting. They were standing a few hundred metres away, huddled together suspiciously and glancing occasionally in my direction. My imagination started to run wild. Maybe they wanted to shoot me, and were waiting till we were all alone. I had my knife, and started to think how I would have to get close enough to the guy with the rifle to make my move if he attacked. I could bury them in the surrounding bush and cross back over the border at night.

"Stop! For Christ's sake!" I told myself. What the hell was I thinking?

But the fact was it was starting to look as though I had been cheated, and I needed to do something quick.

It was time to be proactive and play them at their own game. I phoned the immigration office in Lubumbashi and explained I would like to speak to somebody in English.

"Ce n'est pas pas possible," came the reply.

"My name is Mr. Richards, and I am a diplomat working at the British Embassy in Kinshasa. There will be a big problem if I cannot speak to somebody," I lied trying to put on an aristocratic accent. There was silence, followed by nervous mutterings.

"Good morning Mr. Richardson, how can I help you?" came the reply in perfect English.

I continued: " I understand you have the passport of a Mr. Philip Harwood there. Mr. Harwood is a personal friend of the British Prime Minister, Tony Blair."

Silence.

"He needs his passport urgently and is worried that it may have been stolen, which if it has, I'm sure I don't need to tell you, will cause very serious problems for your office."

The next day my passport arrived on a private aircraft with a six-month visa. If you can't beat them, join them.

★ ★ ★

At last I was ready to go, but not before I was told the South African pilot who flew in my passport wanted to speak to me about paddling the Luvua River.

"Ag man, why the fuck do you wanna go into that area for," he spat. You could tell he was old school Afrikaans. His name was Pete, dishevelled looking, deeply tanned, unshaven and with fingers like bananas. I explained why I was here.

"You know it's pretty fucking wild in there man, I've worked out here for fucking years man, fought in the war. Believe me I know what I'm talking about."

Was he the real deal or a bullshitter?

He continued: "Do you know there's still Mai Mai rebels in there? It's so fucking wild nobody goes there, and they're still armed man. I'm telling you if they catch you, they'll kill you, and it wont be a quick death."

"I don't want to hear this. You're not helping me."

I meant it.

"No bullshit, I'm telling you, a year ago two Belgian missionaries were captured, tortured, and had their balls cut off and eaten. Then their heads were cut off and put on spikes outside their village."

He also then went on to tell me how a couple of years earlier, three South African kayakers had tried to paddle the Luvua, and a week later he had to fly in there in his chopper and collect two of their drowned bodies. The other guy was never found.

To be honest I could have punched him. This was the last thing I wanted to hear, but he fetched over some local officials to confirm the story, and they all shook their heads, looking very serious indeed. I decided I didn't like him.

"Fuck it!" I blurted out, looking him in the eye. "I don't wanna hear any more." I was getting angry. "I've come a long way to do this, and I'm not going to give up now. Fuck the Mai Mai, I'm still going. End of story."

They looked at each other and shrugged their shoulders.

"Okay, Okay. It's your life. Good luck," he said.

★ ★ ★

The night before I left, I paid a visit to Xavier at his home, and even though he was the headman in charge of the naval garrison here, he lived in a simple mud hut with a straw roof. We sat outside overlooking the lake and drinking tea, and it again hit home to me how lucky we are in the West. This guy had a wife and three kids, and he hadn't been paid for six months, and at no point had he ever asked me for any money. I gave him some T-shirts and some toy cars for his kids that I had bought back in Lusaka. He almost looked tearful when we said our goodbyes.

THE LUVUA

Uncharted Territory

The next morning I took my canoe out of the armoury. To my disgust, I discovered that a low down dirty rat had eaten part of my buoyancy aid. What was it with rats in the Congo? Fourteen years earlier on my trans-Africa trip a rat had eaten half an inner tube. I remember finding it in my spares box bloated with a little fat stomach, lying on its back looking rather pleased with itself, just before it bit me as I tried to chuck it out. My medical book said if you get bitten, you should keep the offending creature for five days and that if it dies during that time you might have rabies. We kept it in a box and fed it on scraps. It died 5 days later, but luckily for me there was no frothing of the mouth on my part.

The map I had of the Luvua River was fairly useless, and after Banana Fingers had scared me half to death, I knew I needed to improve my chances. As luck would have it, on the wall of the immigration boss's office there was an aerial photo of the Luvua River area made by a mining company. It wasn't brilliant, but it was a lot better than anything I had, so I insisted the bloke sell it to me, and wouldn't take no for an answer. I paid $100 for it in the end. Totally ripped off. But for what I was about to do it was worth its weight in gold.

★ ★ ★

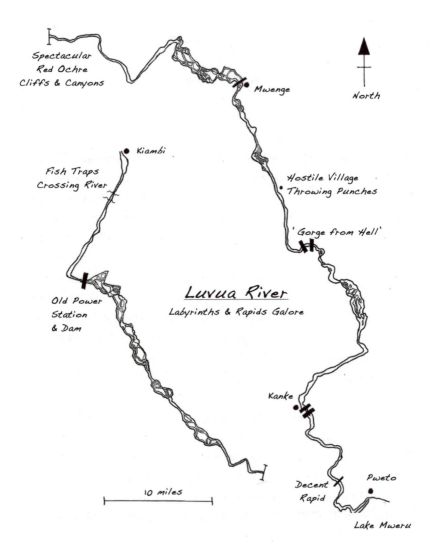

Spectacular
Red Ochre
Cliffs & Canyons

Mwenge

North

Kiambi

Fish Traps
Crossing River

Hostile Village
Throwing Punches

'Gorge from Hell'

Luvua River
Labyrinths & Rapids Galore

Old Power
Station
& Dam

Kanke

10 miles

Decent
Rapid

Pweto

Lake Mweru

It was great to be back on the river again; fast water, hills either side, and after half an hour I was into some rapids. Often it was simply a case of making a choice between the inside or outside of a bend. If I got it wrong I might just get a fright, with some water in the boat, or have to paddle like stink for the bank, then get out and scout ahead. I got it wrong at one point and had to quickly ram myself into a wall of reeds so as not to get swept over a small rocky waterfall. This is when the rope came in handy and I could use it to lower down my canoe.

I'd had no idea the landscape here would look like this. Golden coloured grass covered the surrounding hills, and occasional abandoned huts built from rocks clung precariously to the steep sided banks. There were large trees that seemed to be covered by giant sheets of white silk blowing in the wind – in reality they were gargantuan house sized spiders webs. On one occasion while trying to sneak around a nasty rapid, I inadvertently brushed against one and was instantly covered in a million spiders. Crawling in my mouth, my ears, up my nose, it was horrible. I'd have screamed like a little girl if I hadn't been such a rugged adventurer type; or at least, if a fisherman hadn't been sitting on a rock watching me. I tried to pull myself together. Luckily they were quite small. Any bigger and I'd have died of a heart attack on the spot. In the end I had to jump into the water to get them all off, but I was finding them in the canoe for the rest of the day. Not good considering I'm scared of the little bleeders. Give me a madman with a machete any day.

A truth was beginning to become apparent. Local knowledge wasn't always what it was cracked up to be concerning the capabilities of my canoe. On one hand it might save my life, on the other, when they told me it was impossible to paddle certain rapids, I had to take the advice with a pinch of salt. These guys had never seen a modern plastic canoe, and therefore had no idea what they were capable of handling. Villagers would often gather on the banks and watch in horror as I paddled certain rapids, then all cheer when I made it okay.

The word 'Kanke' had come up time and time again in Pweto. This was apparently the first waterfall of note on route. It turned out to be a series of dangerous rapids and smaller waterfalls split by an island in the middle of the river. Probably okay for expert kayakers, but not by little old me in my canoe. A crowd of guys offered to help carry my canoe around the falls, and I picked a chilled-out older guy to be in charge. He turned out to be a great character.

After half an hour or so of walking around some serious multiple waterfalls we arrived at a substantial village. A fellow with a seriously furrowed brow dressed in rags, announced himself as the local immigration chief. Something unique to the Congo was that there were immigration officials everywhere. Other countries only had them on the borders, but here, even the smallest of settlements you would find a guy with a white shirt and black beret. I'm sure some of them were bogus, but the majority of them were not, and it didn't make life particularly easy for foreigners like me.

This guy insisted I wait while he put on his uniform, slung his AK47 over his shoulder and tidied his mud hut complete with desk and chair. He then seemed to relax as he got into his stride of explaining to me the charges I would need to pay him. For a short while his furrowed brow even relaxed. But when I informed him I wouldn't pay, you could have done your laundry on his washboard forehead.

"What do you mean you wont pay? You must pay," he said

furiously, poking my shoulder with his finger. He then grabbed me by both shoulders and gave me a little shake before adding: "You are very lucky I do not get physical with you." He looked me up and down with disgust. "I am trying to be nice, to show you hospitality, and you insult me."

I couldn't help laughing out loud, which made him even angrier. I reckoned his bark was worse than his bite.

"You are also lucky you did not get physical," I said. It was also all talk, but I was sure I had this guy sussed, and it seemed to do the trick.

I stood up and offered him a few cigarettes before walking out. He was a sod, and the old guy who helped me earlier raised his eyebrows and shook his head in disgust to confirm this.

* * *

Various fishermen had warned me about some dangerous water coming up over the course of the next couple of days. I presumed either some rapids or a waterfall; and sure enough the banks of the river were starting to become rockier and steeper. I eventually came across a large left-hand bend in the river, with the beginnings of broken vertical cliffs either side, and the water picking up speed. Suddenly I noticed some frantically waving fishermen on the left-hand bank. They were either saying hello or were trying to warn me of something. I paddled in and was very glad I did.

You didn't need to understand the lingo to work out what they were trying to say. "Whatever you do, don't go around the corner," seemed to be the gist of it. I bowed to their wisdom – and conveniently for them they made a few dollars out of it, helping me carry my canoe around.

I was itching to get a look at the rapids, but they insisted the easiest route was away from the cliffs. Though it was lush green by the river, as we steadily climbed up and around, the greenery gave way to a bone dry stunted forest with not a leaf in sight.

As I struggled and sweated up the hill, a lizard ran across the path and drew my eyes to the thing that had probably killed the South African kayakers I had heard about from Banana Fingers back in Pweto. Through the trees about a kilometre away, was the canyon from hell. With vertical rock cliffs either side, it culminated in a horrendous shoot of turbulent water a hundred metres across, and I remember thinking no craft could survive that. I've rafted on the Zambezi, the White Nile and in the Himalayas, but this was certain death. I reckon the kayakers got to the bend, ignored the locals advice, got sucked into the canyon and that was it.

Always seek local knowledge.

Whilst walking around I was also treated to a welcome like no other, in a village as far removed from the West as you could imagine. Set on top of a small hill, with a two thousand foot high rock escarpment as a backdrop, it was reminiscent of an old Tarzan film. There were totally traditional huts with straw roofs and the whole village turned out to greet me. There must have been a hundred people, all healthy looking, and all wanting me to take a picture of them as a village. After the bizarre photo shoot, I went one better and showed them their faces on the video LCD screen. They went crazy and absolutely loved it. At no time did anybody ask me for anything or any money. The humble fishermen in these wild places were without doubt the best thing about the trip. Unfortunately there was always an exception to this rule, as I was to discover the next day.

The areas in between the rapids and falls were where people were most likely to have never seen a Mazungu. It was in one such stretch of river, totally cut off from the outside world, where, for the first time on the trip, I honestly thought my time was up. Bizarrely, what I remember most about the whole incident was a limping duck.

I hadn't seen anyone all day and I was paddling along, minding my own business, when I surprised some women washing their clothes.

"Jambo, habari," I blurted out, but it was too late. They dropped everything and sprinted off into the bush screaming. I felt a bit guilty, as all their clothes were now lying in the mud. I thought I'd wander off down the track and make amends. After a couple of minutes, I was confronted by the chief, catapult in hand, looking pretty nervous. He was about half my size and seemed understandably confused. I launched into my smiley hand shaking greetings routine, which seemed to chill him out a bit and he invited me back to his village.

The first thing I noticed was the limping duck, waddling about in the background. As the village gathered around, and after I'd finished the initial pleasantries and my Swahili ran out, they sent for the only guy in the village who spoke some French. To cut a long story short, the communication became a bit of a problem, because the French speaker who probably had bragged to all and sundry of his linguistic skills, turned out to be full of shit, and hardly spoke a word. The trouble was they all started to get a little bit angry that I apparently couldn't speak French or Swahili. I managed to deduce from their body language and the odd words, that they thought that this ignorance was unacceptable and insulting. When I suggested that I could speak French and their man couldn't (bad move), the atmosphere quickly degenerated. I was surrounded by a group of muscle-bound blokes, all shouting and sneering. But as if in a trance, I felt my attention drawn again to the limping duck plodding around in the background, oblivious to the poor Mazungu who was about to get lynched. I imagined what he'd be doing in a couple of hours after I had gone, and whether he was for meat or eggs. Either way he seemed pretty chilled now amongst the shouting and screaming. All I wanted was some god damn peace too.

My gut feeling told me it was time to leave, and I quickly stood up, noticing as I did that a few of the guys backed away. I announced it was time for me to go and said my farewells and thanks in the best Swahili I could muster. I'm sure they were all great people, but for some reason these circumstances and the mob

97

mentality seemed to bring out the worst in many of them, and I really had the impression they wanted to do me in.

The utter contempt and disgust on some of their faces reminded me not to look scared. As I walked down the path back to the river the men eagerly followed, walking backwards in front of me, surrounding me, staring at my face for any indication of fear, and shouting god knows what. One guy walked up to me and threw a couple of fake punches at my face to see if I'd flinch. I didn't and threw one back. He stumbled and fell over. It still felt like they might all turn violent any second. I had my knife on my belt, but in reality it was ten to one, and I wouldn't have stood a chance. Within a couple of seconds of reaching the riverbank, I leapt into my canoe and the weight carried me straight out into the river.

There's nowt as queer as folk.

★ ★ ★

By way of contrast, that same afternoon, after negotiating a maze of channels and easy rapids, I met some of the loveliest people you could hope to meet. It was a small family settlement; probably five to eight people. After exchanging waves from across the river I tried to paddle across the current to get to them but it was too strong and I got swept downstream. I camped about a mile further on, in the bush. An hour later, they turned up, having tramped all the way through the bush because they thought I was in trouble and needed help. We sat around my fire and I gave them a bag of rice, for which they were very grateful.

One guy warned me about the rapids downstream, and insisted he and his brother guide me around them. At dawn the next morning we set off, and sure enough if I had gone the wrong way I'd have probably been smashed on the rocks. But theses blokes had been brought up fishing these waters and knew every inch of every channel at each different time of the year. I was particularly impressed by the way they used their long poles, to skilfully negotiate their way through the tiny islands and rapids. Standing either end of their dugout – which must have been only a couple of feet wide – they were totally at one with the environment, and at no time looked unbalanced.

★ ★ ★

I found a great camp spot a couple of nights later. The river had again widened up with lots of channels and little islands and I was quite enjoying trying to find my way through it all. The rapids were frequent but never too scary, and only once did I screw up and end up somewhere I shouldn't have been: a sharp corner with lots of white water and impenetrable jungle either side. There was no way of knowing what was around the corner without committing myself to the current, and as it was quite powerful water, once you were in there was no going back. If it flattened out, great, but if it got worse, not great. It took me about an hour to paddle back upstream to where I found an alternative route. On most other rivers I've paddled especially in Britain, there's nearly always somewhere to get out on the bank and walk along the bank for a look. But here that was often not an option, since thick unpleasant jungle created an impenetrable wall of foliage right down into the water.

The camp spot was right in the middle of all this, with a handy raised rock platform to sleep on. There was fast clean water on three sides and some virgin jungle and plenty of firewood behind. No sooner had I set up than I heard some creature moving about in the bush behind, saw an eagle soaring overhead and a couple of otters were playing nearby. I could feel an anchovy night coming on.

Whenever I go on a big trip somewhere, my mum always sends me a tin or two of anchovies as a treat. I stick them in the bottom of my bag for either a special occasion or when I'm feeling a bit down. This spot was worthy of my little salty friends. I never did find out what critter was in the bush, but I had a great night's kip.

***

Mwenge was the only main village on my map before Kiambi, and from talking to the fishermen I'd learned that it also had a nasty rapid. Even the map showed a line across the river, which meant something substantial. But when you ask three different fishermen in the space of half an hour, and you get answers with between one hour and eight hours difference, it pays to stay open minded.

In Mwenge itself the whole village turned out to see me as usual, and a large hut was made available for me to meet the elders. All but one seemed pretty chilled, especially the chief, and they all agreed that paddling the rapids was not an option. The only guy who took a dislike to me was the village policeman (or so he claimed to be). He was barefooted with torn shorts and a blue jacket, but he carried his rusty AK47 with pride, holding it out in front of him when he spoke. Occasionally he'd butt in and suggest I pay loads of money. The others, if anything, seemed a bit embarrassed by him. When we eventually found some willing porters and set off, he came along, and after we got to the river he insisted I pay him for being my security. I paid him bugger all.

The map showed many channels and islands after Mwenge and sure enough it didn't disappoint. The hardest thing for me as usual was not having a clue which way to go, or what the water was like. Too many times I had been told it was flat, only to be sucked into a jungle of white-water, and other times bracing myself for hell, it turned out to be a doddle.

Fortunately the rapids were mostly easy on this section, and when they weren't there was always a way around. There were indeed hundreds of islands and channels, and as this challenge was becoming a regular one, I was starting to get used to it and enjoying the exploratory feel of it all. One of the most important skills I think you can have as a river paddler is the ability to read the water and the landscape for an indication of what's coming up. And I was certainly getting lots of practice on this trip. Who needs guide books anyway?

When it finally all opened out and became one river again, I spent the night in one of the poorest villages I came across on the trip. Flanked by walls of ten foot high elephant grass, the river was now wide and shallow, and surrounded as far as the eye could see by towering ochre coloured mountains. With only an hour before dark, I had been invited to spend the night in the village of a fisherman I had met whilst paddling. His French was excellent (probably because his name was Pierre), but I couldn't help feeling sorry for him. For a start he looked exhausted. He had a sad look on his face as though he had resigned himself to a life of extreme poverty and suffering. As he led me up to his village, I didn't dare ask him if my canoe would be safe left on the bank. I felt he might be offended and take it as an insult on his character. When we got to the village and I met some of the people, something told me my canoe wouldn't be touched, as they were all so respectful.

The village consisted of a large dustbowl of a square, surrounded by a dozen or so scraggy huts. I don't think people had the energy to come running over to see who I was. Everybody was really gently spoken and humble, but there wasn't an ounce of fat on any of them. A lot of the kids were naked with bloated stomachs from malnutrition.

Not long after arriving I was sitting around the campfire chatting to the chief in the flickering light. I often felt guilty when I was cooking my food, and the problem was never more pressing than usual here. Everybody just sat and stared. All I had was a pot of rice and one flat tin of sardines, but as far as they were concerned it was a banquet. In the end I couldn't bear it any longer and gave the chief a large bag of rice. His eyes nearly popped out of his head. Then I gave him a full pack of cigarettes to share around, and soon the mood had changed with staring being replaced by laughter and banter. It felt good.

Everything would have been perfect if it hadn't been for the chief of the next village who suddenly turned up drunk, and gave the local headman a bollocking for not informing him of my arrival. To make matters worse he then tried to confiscate the cigarettes for himself, forcing me to step in and tell him off, ordering him to give the cigarettes back. In the end it all calmed down and I had a great night's sleep under the stars – even though I had diarrhoea like a hosepipe.

In the morning I gave the nice chief a big roll of fishing line and some hooks for the village and it was the first time I saw him really smile.

★ ★ ★

If you've forked out the money to buy this book, you might be somebody like me who loves looking at maps of far-flung places. Back in Britain, often on a rainy day with some tea and toast at hand, I spent countless hours studying every inch of my Congo maps. I was always trying to picture what it would actually look like on the ground, and trying to guess whether the river was a millpond or a raging torrent. John Blashford Snell's 1974 Zaire River Expedition had left some really handy maps of rapids on the Lualaba, but I hadn't been able to find anything on the Luvua River.

On one long straight section on the Luvua, the map showed that the river narrowed quite considerably, and I must admit to being a bit nervous of what was there, expecting a horrendously long gorge from hell, with an equally horrendous portage. As it turned out it was absolutely idyllic. Two thousand foot high escarpments rose up both sides and the river narrowed to less than a hundred metres, but the water was like a millpond. No villages, no fishermen; I had it all to myself, and very nice it was too. The hillsides were covered with strange, gnarled and twisted leafless stunted trees again, dry as a bone. Only by the river was there greenery. Soaring ochre coloured cliffs added to the mix and made it quite memorable. This went on for pretty much the whole day before the hills subsided and the water quickened.

After a couple more days of small rapids and numerous channels, I came across something rather out of place. On one of the maps, there was a line across the river representing some falls or a substantial rapid. Instead of those – and totally unexpectedly – I came across an old dam and disused power station. Everything was totally overgrown. First came a pretty basic rusted solid dam with a walkway across the top, followed by a narrow canal and then a path leading to a village on the left. A decent sized village came next with a bloody great power station in disrepair next to the river below. Higher up it was a boiling mass of water in a narrow rocky gorge, gradually losing ferocity the further it travelled from the main dam.

I found a couple of guys to help me carry the canoe around, but was soon being followed by a growing crowd of followers, a bit like the Pied Piper, until finally an official shouted for me to stop. He loved the fact that he had a large audience.

"Follow me Mazungu, you need my permission to be here. You must pay for a permit." He was pissed and slurring his words.

I wasn't in the mood to play his silly games.

"I'm sorry but you're drunk and I don't deal with drunk people," I said before walking off. Everybody burst out laughing, except for Mr… whatever his name was.

"The police will arrest you. You are in big trouble Mazungu!" he barked, and followed alongside getting more and more aggravated.

A nice sober official then turned up.

"Please Mazungu, you should go with him. He is an important man."

All I wanted to do was get on the damn river. I could see the narrow chute of white water below, and was trying to work out if I could paddle it safely. The longer I walked around, the more grief I was going to get. But there was no way any of them would follow me on the river.

"Down here," I said to my helpers, and we changed direction down to the river.

"You can't put on here it is too dangerous," the nice one said.

"I'll be okay. Thanks for your help," I said shaking his hand.

The entire river was no more than 10 metres wide having come straight out of the dam a little further upstream. It was a bit hairy with some powerful boils but I thought as long as I stayed in the middle it should be fine. The large crowd went completely silent as I got on, but when they realised I was in control, they cheered as I punched through some of the large standing waves. I was free again.

The only other obstacle the next day was line upon line of fish traps, spanning virtually the entire river like sort of scaffolding tank traps. As the unopposed central chute was often a bit dodgy, I'd find myself manhandling my canoe either through or over the inconvenient structures. Not the end of the world, but bloody hard work.

★ ★ ★

Eight days after leaving Pweto, I arrived at the village of Kiambi. After travelling through some truly wild country, my genitals and head were still intact. But almost more importantly my determination to make it to the Atlantic Ocean had taken a step forward.

Of all the sections of the Congo River, I am most proud of having paddled this section, as some of it was true exploring. I met some hostility from locals, but I think that's to be expected in a country that's been so brutalised and exploited. Most of this hostility was really fear of the unknown, and after people realised I was friendly and willing to sit and chat, they relaxed. Where the fishing was good, the men were built like brick outhouses and very healthy looking indeed – but occasionally I'd come across a village miles from anywhere, that was teetering between life and death.

On these occasions I'd end up giving away food and medicine, as they needed it a lot more than I did.

Kiambi wasn't anything to write home about, but I had an ulterior motive for wanting to stop here. Back in Lusaka I had met an Irish guy who told me he worked for an NGO in Manono, a town not a million miles away from Kiambi, and that if I ever made it this far (which he didn't think I would) I should go and visit him. After a couple of days of waiting for a passing motorbike, I was fortunate (or unfortunate) enough to meet Henri with his 500cc trial bike; a great guy. It took us an hour to get to Manono, with me hanging on the back for dear life. Most of the trail was about three feet wide in thick bush with loads of deep sand. And, if you didn't already know, the only way to ride a motorbike on deep sand is FLAT OUT!

The river at times was scary enough, but that ride brought a whole new level of fear. Henri was clearly brilliant on his motorbike, but a certified loon, and we inevitably crashed, requiring me to leap into the air to prevent my legs getting trapped. It felt a bit crazy really because I had worked so hard to stay alive so far, using my own skills and experience to take calculated risks, and here I was putting my life completely in the hands of a total stranger. But I must admit I quite enjoyed the adrenaline rush.

We only stopped once, to top up his leaking oil reservoir, and some guys soon closed in to try to sell me some booze. One of them told me to buy him a bottle, and when I refused he got really pissed off.

"You refuse me?" he asked angrily looking around at his mates.

"Bloody cheek!" I thought. Who the hell did he think he was? But these didn't look like the sort of guys you wanted to play monopoly with, and luckily I was able to make a quick get away on my trusty steed.

The Irish guy was away when I arrived, and a beautiful raven haired, southern Irish girl met me instead. Her name was Catherine, and she gave me my own room for a couple of days.

They had a buffet meal three times a day, a working fridge for cold drinks, and my double bed had crisp white sheets. It was without doubt the most luxurious three days of the entire trip, and a great opportunity to recharge my batteries.

Manono is the largest town on the road (if you can call it a road) between Lubumbashi and Kalemie, and even has an airport. It was once the toast of the mining community with its wonderfully planned streets and local amenities, but was now almost completely deserted. Most of the buildings were overgrown and in ruins. Apparently the surrounding area contains one hundred million tonnes of tin and columbite, but thanks to both the collapse of the world's tin prices in the 1980s, and the destruction caused by the Second Congo War, the town was now a shadow of its former self.

The UN carried out arms decommissioning in 2008, offering to accept guns in exchange for bicycles. There was an abundance of people cycling around the place, so it seems to have done the trick. There's even a cathedral built by the Belgians in the town centre, but it too was badly damaged in the war and was boarded up with most of the windows smashed and the spire in a real state. I even found an old public swimming pool completely overgrown, empty and abandoned to the elements. Buildings in the dirt high street still had the original signs above the door: butcher, boulangerie, pharmacy – but they were now one and the same, all selling rice, blankets and other imported goods.

In 2003 due to the humanitarian disaster caused by the Mai Mai rebels moving south, the town was made a base of operations by MONUC (French for: United Nations Observer Mission in DR Congo). Soon after this the NGOs started moving in. The UN base around the corner, with its watch towers, razor wire and armed guards, provided some degree of security, but corruption was still rife – as I was to find out.

It doesn't take long for word to get around that there is a new foreigner in town and sure enough the next morning, Catherine (there is something about a southern Irish accent that makes me go all weak at the knees) rather apologetically requested that I go and speak to the immigration leeches (her words). They wanted to grill the new meat. After three hours sweating in their rundown office, I started to lose my mild mannered composure at their explanation of why I needed to pay them money.

"Look. I know the government doesn't pay you much, but I am not a walking bank," I said. They were nice guys, and for that reason everything had remained pleasant.

"Ten months," one of them said. "We haven't been paid for ten months."

"I've met some guys who haven't been paid for years," I said. "Maybe you need to look for another job."

But I knew jobs were scarce.

They wanted me to really understand some fine point that I hadn't quite grasped in French, and took me on the back of a motorbike to the UN headquarters to speak to an interpreter. Surrounded by watchtowers, the officers were all sitting in their lounge watching football on Sky TV. I thought back to the contrast a few days earlier, when I had been hacking my way through the bush. Surprise, surprise, their intricate point turned out to be complete rubbish, with me apparently not realising I had to pay immigration to enter the country. Hello! I was already *in* the country.

"Every country I've ever been to, you pay once on entering, and you might pay again when you leave. That's it!" I was beginning to rant.

"Ah yes, but you have only been here for about a week. Manono is an important town. Everybody else pays."

He seemed to have convinced himself.

"For one thing, I'm not everybody else, and if I paid money in every village or town that asked for it, I'd end up starving to death."

I looked at the Moroccan captain for support. He reluctantly tore himself away from the football match. "He is right", he said.

"In Morocco you pay once on entry and that's it. He cannot pay in every town."

"Just in this town. I am hungry," he cut to the chase.

"Bloody cheek," I thought.

The captain shrugged his shoulders and waved us away, he had important business on the TV. I got up and walked out, closely followed by my entourage. Back in their little office they continued their barrage, but when they finally started raising their voices, I realised that I don't need this shit, got up and walked out. They started following, but soon gave up.

★ ★ ★

I felt like a new man after three days in Manono, and staying at Catherine's outfit at ten dollars a night it was the best value pick me up I've ever had. I had stashed my canoe in an old guys hut back in Kiambi, his job was to paddle people across the river. After just about surviving the motorbike ride back by the skin of my teeth, I was soon back on the river, full of energy. The crisp white sheets of Manono soon became a distant dreamy memory.

THE MIDDLE LUALABA

Malaria, Chased and Arrested

For many years, geographers have argued over the source of the River Congo. Today, there are still some who believe the Lualaba is the source due to its relatively bigger volume over the Luvua. If we assume, however, that the longest tributary is the source, then the way I had come, via the Chambeshi, Luapula and the Luvua win hands down. Ankoro is the village at the junction point of the Luvua and Lualaba rivers, and as I passed here the Luvua was clearly the larger river at three times the width of the Lualaba. Seeing it at first hand, that is was clearly a bigger river than the Lualaba, got me so excited I nearly fell out of my boat. My mind was racing. I'll be famous, a world-renowned explorer, and rich beyond my wildest dreams. Women will travel hundreds of miles just to catch a glimpse of the famous adventurer, hoping to slip their phone number into my hand. Paddling all day in the stifling heat was taking its toll!

The town of Kabalo was next up, and I didn't want to attract attention and show off my pale skinned good looks. In hindsight I should have paddled past at night; as it was I opted for the camouflage of an early morning mist. I hugged the opposite bank.

Surely they would all be tucked up in bed? As I drew level I could make out huge rusting warehouses, cranes and railway carriages. Some women were washing their clothes and babies in the river, but it was the hurried activity that caught my eye. Four

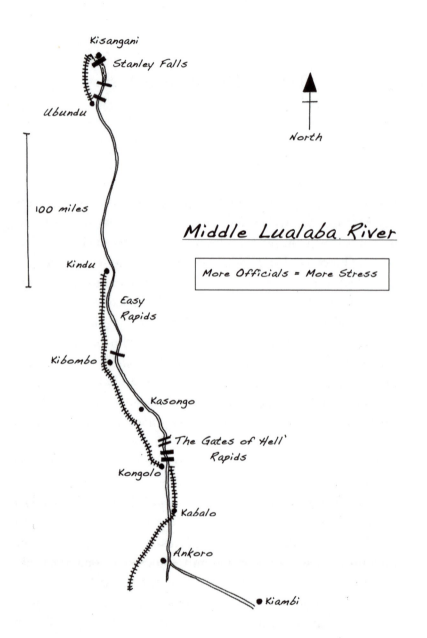

Kisangani
Stanley Falls
Ubundu

North

100 miles

Kindu

Middle Lualaba River

More Officials = More Stress

Easy
Rapids

Kibombo

Kasongo

The Gates of Hell'
Rapids

Kongolo

Kabalo

Ankoro

Kiambi

110

men were frantically boarding two dugout canoes, before paddling hard out into the river ahead of me. At least they weren't heading for me, I thought. I noticed they were wearing soldier's uniforms at about the same time one of them shouted Mazungu. Was there no peace to be had in this godforsaken land? They were trying to cut me off at the pass, and simply turned and waited.

When I refused their demands to go ashore and tried to paddle off, one of them picked up his AK47. I got the hint. By the time they had persuaded me, we were already a couple of hundred metres past the town, and I had to paddle hard against the current to get back – which really pissed me off. I was getting a bit tired of all this and wasn't in the mood to be humble.

Waiting below a towering, rusted solid crane was a large contingent of Kabalo's finest, comprising the army, immigration and custom bosses surrounded by their lackeys. It didn't look good, but I still went into my smiling, meeting and greeting routine, explaining myself and showing my passport and letters of authority.

From past experience, I knew that the way I conducted myself was often a big factor in how I would be treated. If I looked and behaved in a cool, calm and collected way, I stood a good chance of not being mucked about. But if I looked even a little bit nervous and intimidated, I would be like a lamb to the slaughter, and I'd get fleeced. Somehow they must have known I was coming. For all these people to be on the riverbank so early in the morning was too much of a coincidence. It didn't look good.

The customs chief was the first to make his move and he asked me what I had in the canoe. When I started to explain he rudely interrupted and ordered me to show him everything, his voice increasing in volume. I paused, staring at him, trying to keep my cool. He wore an obscenely loud Hawaiian shirt, and his look smacked of utter contempt. This alone made me want to punch him in the face. As about twenty people surrounded me, I slowly took out my barrel and rucksack showing him the contents.

"Take out everything," he ordered, pointing at my foam buoyancy, which concealed my hidden compartments for the medical kit and camera boxes.

"Why?" I asked. "This is not a border, I don't have to do this."

He lurched closer, along with some others, sensing defiance, like a pack of wolves eager for a chance to pounce. Goddamn leeches.

"There's too many people here. I'll show you, but not in front of all this lot," I said, fighting not to lose my patience.

He waved away the minions, leaving only the privileged few. I grumpily revealed all. He waved for me to give him the camera case. I refused, offering only him a look, using my body to shield it from the others. He tried to take out my cameras, but I said no and he seemed satisfied for now. I packed everything away. Then came the crux.

"Empty your pockets and take off your shirt," he said with a deadpan expression. I froze and stared at him, incredulous, looking deep into his eyes, searching for information as to the size of his balls. His eyes wavered, that was enough.

"No chance," I said calmly. The army guy lunged towards me.

"You try! Come on … try," I sneered splaying my arms out like a pumped up football hooligan. He froze. I was on the verge of losing it. If he laid a hand on me, at least I'd go down fighting. I'd had enough of this shit. All my cash was hidden from view around my waist and – as I may have mentioned, if there was one thing I didn't like it was people manhandling me. Everything seemed to freeze for about ten seconds… Enough time for me think.

"What are you looking for anyway?" I eventually asked.

"A gun," said the soldier, who actually had a nice enough face.

I asked one of the other soldiers to come forward and put his hands in the air, which he did. They looked confused. I then gave a demonstration of how to search somebody for a gun, explaining that I'd be happy to let 'nice faced' soldier man pat me down. They agreed and he found nothing.

Fifteen minutes later I was sitting in the tiny mud brick immigration office where I was informed my visa was no good and I needed both a new photography and a new travel permit. Luckily for me everything could be sorted out for the bargain price of a hundred dollars. Same old story.

Two hours later, they still hadn't got their pound of flesh and decided to try something else. The immigration guy asked for another look at my passport, and as I handed it to him he stood up, put it in his back pocket and said: "When you pay the hundred dollars, I'll give you it back." Then he began to walk out.

Luckily I was between him and the doorway, and instinctively stood up and kicked the doorframe hard leaving my leg there, preventing him from leaving. Some mud fell from the ceiling.

"You're not going anywhere till you give my passport back," I growled jabbing my finger in his chest. He sat down on his desk looking a little bit stunned, then shouted to somebody outside to fetch the police. If there had been a mirror on the wall, I'd have looked at it to check I didn't have the word 'MUG' tattooed on my forehead. Who the hell did this guy think he was?

I thought back to an incident that occurred whilst driving my Land Rover to Cape Town. We were following an English couple in their Range Rover driving along a beautiful beach in Mauritania. They were great people, but not very worldly wise. They were stopped by a couple of soldiers and as we waited behind them they suddenly started handing over a wad of cash through the window. I instantly jumped out and ran over, demanding to know what was going on. After a feeble excuse from the soldiers, I demanded they hand the money back, which they did.

The words fear, intimidation and opportunism spring to mind when I think about it. Fear from the western world, as a result of how they perceive Africa to be, due to the constant doom and gloom from the media. Intimidation from some, who are not stupid and very clearly understand and recognise the nervousness of the average outsider, and the possible rewards to be had. And lastly opportunism, I believe partly born from generations of handouts from westerners assuaging their guilt at hundreds of years of earlier exploitation and barbarism. It's habit forming to take, and a lot easier too. When you've got a corrupt government that doesn't give a hoot about its people, you can see why we westerners are often regarded as too good a money making opportunity to let pass by.

Back in Kabalo, the situation didn't look good. I knew I was pushing my luck, but I was fed up with being bullied. When three policemen turned up, I decided to stand my ground.

"Arrest this man," ordered the immigration guy. "Take him away."

The nearest policeman tugged gently at my sleeve. "Come with me," he said, his obvious unease fuelling my defiance.

"No. This man has stolen my passport. I want you to arrest him," I countered using the opportunity to practice my scary look. He didn't know what to do.

After five minutes of this stand off, the police chief turned up, and his eyes told me to tread very carefully indeed. You don't get to be a police chief in the Congo by sending everybody Christmas cards. This guy looked like he meant business. Before he could open his mouth, I took the initiative and offered another alternative.

"Hello. This man has taken my passport and won't give it back till I give him a hundred dollars," I explained calmly. "I'm happy to come with you, when he returns my passport." Following a conversation in Swahili that was too quick for me to understand, my passport was returned and I was taken away.

The police station, like most other government buildings in the Congo was a partial ruin; a neglected remnant of the sixties. At least the Chiefs office had a decent roof. I sat on a lonely stool in the middle of the room as he studied me from behind his desk. A picture of president Joseph Kabila was on the wall behind him, and the room was bare apart form the two chairs and his table. The police chief was probably in his late forties, and looked pretty healthy despite being overweight. With tribal scars on his face and forearms and deep sunken eyes, he looked very tough, and I hoped things didn't get ugly. I didn't relish the idea of getting him in a headlock. God knows what he'd pull out of his pocket.

I had two thousand five hundred dollars in cash hidden secretly in my belt. All my important documents and another five hundred cash in a waterproof pouch hanging around my neck under my clothes, and two hundred cash both U.S and local francs spread throughout various pockets, some hidden.

"What's that around your neck?" he asked, far too quietly.

"Its just some documents," I said. "Nothing important."

"Let me see," he said, suddenly smiling broadly and raising his eyebrows; giving his own solo performance of good cop, bad cop. I handed him a wad of cards and papers to inspect but left the money inside. He went through every item asking what it was for before looking very concerned about a business card for a mining guy I knew who worked in Kolwezi. He was an ex-French Foreign Legionnaire.

"This is not good," he said solemnly. "Big trouble for you."

I felt like saying, "Oh fuck off you idiot," but instead laughed and explained it was from a chance meeting in Lusaka. I think he was starting to realise I knew the score.

"Show me all your money," he said.

"I'm sorry," I said smiling. "I don't have to do that, and I'm not going to do that." We stared into each other's eyes for a few seconds.

I was taken to the town jail, complete with bars, and full of prostitutes, but the door was open and everyone was sitting around chatting. A particularly large breasted woman in a mini skirt very kindly offered me a seat.

"You will spend the night here," said the Chief studying me for a reaction.

"Fine," I said. "I will practice my Swahili."

I would have loved to say "alright gorgeous" to my new

girlfriend but didn't know how.

He looked disappointed by my indifference, and after an hour I was taken back to immigration.

It was one thing after another, the day was drawing on and my bottle of patience was almost empty. In the end I reluctantly agreed to pay fifty dollars. I just wanted to get back on the river. But it wasn't enough, and believe it or not, after examining my compact camera, he again put it in his pocket and the same thing happened all over again. He tried to leave, my foot went across the door, the police were called and I refused to budge. He then returned it and this time I stormed off to what I believed to be the big boss's office behind the police station.

To cut a long story short, I barged in on Kabalo's head honcho having a meeting with a UN Army officer from Benin. They listened to my tales of woe, but weren't really interested and sniggered to themselves, having a laugh at my expense. So much for the UN. I returned to the immigration office with a police entourage – as he still had my letter of authority from Pweto. I held up a fifty-dollar note and asked for a private chat.

"You give me a new photo and travel permit, valid for the whole country and I'll give you the cash." I paused for a moment before adding: "If you don't take it, I'll give you nothing."

Half an hour later I was back on the river with my new permits. It was an hour before dark.

★ ★ ★

The town of Kongolo was the end of the road as far as riverboats were concerned on this section of the Lualaba; the infamous Gates of Hell put paid to them. This was the name for a fearsome set of rapids directly below the town, and I couldn't wait to get a look.

After the corruption in Kabalo I didn't quite know what to expect in Kongolo, the next village, but luckily for me the first person I met was John, a riverboat captain who turned out to be just what the doctor ordered. In stark contrast to the meatheads the day before, John was the nicest and most genuine bloke you could hope to meet, and he even spoke a bit of English. I would usually get mobbed landing directly on the shore, so I had paddled alongside his riverboat to get some information on a place to stay, and he quickly filled me in on what was what. Within a couple of minutes I knew this was a man I could trust, and, since he wasn't leaving Kongolo for a few days, he agreed to let me stash my canoe on his boat, and refused to take any money.

There was even a guesthouse in town, and he insisted on taking me there himself. Bliss. The day was getting better and better, I couldn't believe it. I had been here for half an hour and I hadn't yet been cornered by soldiers or immigration. But sure as eggs are eggs, when I was shown my room, complete with bed and padlocked door, a couple of shifty looking dudes turned up firing questions at John. And so began a heated debate in a mixture of French and Swahili.

It was pretty clear they wanted their pound of flesh, and John was fighting my corner playing the 'we should be showing hospitality to strangers' card. He must have held some respect in town because it seemed to be working. In the end, all I had to do was go to their office and fill out the ledger and the only excitement was an angry drunk hurling abuse at me.

Mazungu-this and Mazungu-that, he started gesticulating wildly with his arms. He clearly had a grudge about something, and I seemed to be the perfect scapegoat. The others ignored him as we approached their office, but for some reason I saw this as an opportunity to show the officials I wouldn't take any shit, and I walked up to him. My chaperones shouted for me to stop but I just looked him in the eye and offered him my hand to shake, which he gingerly took.

"Hello, my name is Phil from England, what's your name?" I said in my best Swahili not breaking eye contact, and luckily – as I had hoped – he calmed down and we had a little chat. Job done.

The high street was a bit wild west, with dusty potholes and littered with abandoned vehicles in various stages of decay. Engine blocks served as improvised tables and chairs, and rusting trucks as a playground for the kids. Although a lot of the buildings were broken down shells, the original signs from the sixties were often still visible, including a butcher's, a national bank and the town hall. Apparently there was one train a month from further south, and the shops stocked a variety of goods with food being fairly limited.

Kongolo was a perfect example of how President Mobutu's criminal reign had caused the country's infrastructure to collapse. The shore was littered with the rusting, decaying hulks of giant river barges, reminiscent of a bygone age. A large tree growing out of one of the holds served as an example as to how long they had been there. Further inland I discovered a roofless warehouse with three perfectly intact, albeit rusted solid old-fashioned steam engines, abandoned to the elements. The grass in that warehouse must have been six feet high in places, and every now and then I'd come across a pillar drill, or other piece of machinery rusted solid and thought back to what it must have been like in its heyday.

I only stayed a couple of nights eating as much as I could, and wandering around exploring the town. Apparently, it was a bit of a hotspot for buying unrefined diamonds. The only other white guy in town was a South African guy called Dale who also happened to be staying in the same guesthouse. It turned out he was a bit of an entrepreneur, and actually lived in Kalemi on the shores of Lake Tanganyika, where he had a fishing business, amongst other things. His interests inland on this occasion were stockpiling grain for export, but he also had a hand in the diamond business. He was fascinated by my trip and took great pleasure in taking the piss out of the book *Blood River*.

This was a book by the journalist Tim Butcher, who attempted to recreate Henry Morton Stanley's journey down the Congo River. He started in Kalemie, and hitched a motorbike ride to

Kindu, before spending a few days on the river as a passenger in a dugout. He then caught a UN motorboat from Kisangani to Mbandaka before flying to Kinshasa. Dale made the journey himself from Kalemie once a month by motorbike, and thought the guy was a bit of a wet blanket for over dramatising his accomplishments. I agreed, to some extent.

★ ★ ★

As the next section of rapids had a bit of a reputation, I hired a guy with a motorbike and went off downstream in search of a fisherman who knew the river like the back of his hand. In the end everybody suggested I speak to Daniel Mboto, and when I finally found him he agreed to guide me down and around the most dangerous part the next day.

It was my forty-third birthday, and I was about to paddle the Gates of Hell, or La Porte de l'Enfer in French. The history books all said that the river was un-navigable from Kongolo to Kindu, with many sets of rapids after the infamous Gates of Hell. The only expedition I knew of to pass this way was the 1975 Army expedition, led by John Blashford Snell using inflatable rafts and jet boats. Luckily for me they very kindly included some information and maps in their post trip expedition report, for which I was very grateful. If it had been the wet season I'd probably have been swept to my death, but I had purposely planned to be here now, whilst the river was lower.

It was dawn and Daniel hadn't turned up. It was a beautiful morning; quiet, peaceful and lots of people were down by the waters edge, washing clothes and themselves. John, the captain of the houseboat, offered me a cup of tea and we sat chatting on deck watching clumps of water hyacinth drift by. He was leaving that day for Mulongo, three hundred kilometres upstream, and his crew were already loading heavy sacks of grain onboard. You could just hear the mechanic tinkering with his engine down in the engine room.

After an hour I couldn't wait any longer and said my farewells. John insisted I must wait for Daniel but I assured him I'd be okay. We shook hands and I cast off.

You know when very occasionally you experience a feeling of utter contentment and peace? Well, as I lazily let myself drift past the residents of Kongolo, going about their business at the river's edge, with the warm sun on my back, I felt content. And as the people gave way to the red rusting hulks of abandoned river barges, one after another beyond repair... I was finally snapped out of my trance like state by the sound of the rapids ahead and the quickening of the river.

Thankfully the water was fairly low; a couple of feet higher and it would have been a different ball game. Everybody said: whatever you do, go left of the island. Which I did. Then it was a case of finding my way through the rocky labyrinth of channels. It was great fun, challenging, sometimes scary, but very satisfying as I negotiated my way down.

Locals were cheering from the bank as I paddled each set of rapids, and I would often stand up to get a better view of what was ahead. In higher water all the rocky islands would have been covered and there would be nowhere to hide, but with the islands exposed it dissipated the power of the river. At one point the river came together again as one chute and I got out to have a look. It looked pretty clear, with no rocks to hit, but the powerful boils and whirlpools were the biggest so far, and didn't look particularly friendly. Some fishermen had now arrived, and were frantically trying to persuade me to carry my canoe around, but I had already decided to paddle it and was soon back on the water.

When I noticed that the fishermen had now stopped waving, and were just staring motionless with very serious looks on their faces, I started to wonder whether I had made the right decision. But it was too late, there was no turning back, the river had me in its grip.

To make matters worse, like an idiot I had forgotten to put on my buoyancy aid, and as I approached the worst section I felt the fear and doubt creeping in. Out of the corner of my eye I noticed the wreck of an ancient paddle steamer on the rocks. The river was now a surging mass of rising and falling water, and struggling to keep straight I inevitably lost control and was spun around ferociously. Round and around I went, first one way, then the other; it was all I could do just to stay upright. I felt like a giant's plaything. When I was finally through the worst of it, I promised myself I wouldn't underestimate the boils and whirlpools again.

A few miles after Kongolo the people disappeared, and I felt rather pleased with myself, I've paddled the Gates of Hell for Christ's sake! For years I had imagined a raging torrent with hundred foot high cliffs, and in the end it turned out to be a bit of an anti-climax. In high water, however, I'm sure it would have been a different story. After a couple of hours I passed under the Kongolo Bridge; little was I to know what was around the next corner.

One minute there were a million fishermen going about their business, then after the bridge there was nobody, and the river widened with marshy islands everywhere. The hills were also getting steeper either side. It didn't look good, and by the shape of the hills further on it seemed as though the river was being channelled into a narrow section. I decided to climb one of the hills for a better look, and sure enough there was a meaty rapid and more rocks ahead, but I also spotted a tiny channel through the reeds bypassing the dodgy bit. I chose the safer option.

It was only a metre wide in places with lots of little rapids and plenty of rocks. I had to get out and drag the canoe over and around rocks a fair bit, trying not skewer myself on broken branches or getting bitten by the two snakes that surprised me. But when I finally emerged below the main falls, I felt quite pleased with myself for having found a sneaky alternative route.

Although the river here was fifteen metres wide and boily as hell, I paddled a few hundred metres of it until I came across a tight

S-bend that I didn't like the look of. The whole river was now squeezed into a ten meter wide twisting rock corridor and it was time for a short portage. As if they knew it was my birthday, three friendly fishermen emerged from nowhere to give me a hand. They were a trio of son, father and grandfather, and made my life a hell of a lot easier by dragging my canoe around to a picturesque little beach with oodles of firewood.

As darkness fell that night, tucking into my grub, I was treated to an all night light show, as the whole skyline was ablaze on the other side of the river. The grass-covered hills were being burnt to create new farmland, and along with the stars being out in force and the water reflecting the glow of the flames, it was quite a sight – and a night I'll never forget.

* * *

The actual Gates of Hell appeared the next day. An impressive rock monolith a hundred feet high rose out of the water in the middle of the river, flanked by rocky cliffs either side. No mystery where it got its name. Though the water here was quick and fairly boily, it was relatively flat.

I felt pretty pleased with myself after that, and as there was a village round the next corner, I allowed myself the luxury of a couple of guides for the next section. My new helpers Amba and

Rab, reckoned it became flat and one river again after a few hours, so we set off hugging the left hand side and made our way through walls of high reed beds. Gradually we encountered more and more small rapids until they finally capsized their dugout and Amba lost his T-shirt, and nearly the canoe. Dugouts are made of hardwood, and when upside down don't exactly float on the surface. I had to work really hard to hold one end up to stop it sinking. After the second capsize I reckoned they had come far enough. I didn't want them to lose their livelihood. I gave them their money and a spare T-shirt for Amba, noted their advice about where to go next and set off, trying to avoid the jagged rocks protruding from both banks like the teeth of a giant serpent.

The next day, when I knew a dodgy rapid was coming up, I agreed to be guided around it by a couple of fishermen and made it very clear I'd give them the money only when we were the other side of the main rapid. I had been paddling twelve-hour days for a while now and was getting a little bit run down, so as it was getting dark, we agreed to stop in a village for the night. My antisocial side took over and suggested I sleep on a sand bank on the other side of the river to the village. The look on their faces soon made me feel guilty, however, and I relented. But then after meeting the Chief and being totally surrounded and stared at for an hour, despite their warnings of big crocodiles in the area, the need for peace and quiet was too strong and I paddled across to the other side. I was too tired to worry about crocs.

The next morning it soon became clear my guides were not comfortable on fast water, and just when it started to get hairy, they admitted they had never been here before and wanted to turn back. Bloody typical – but fair enough.

The river must have been four hundred metres wide, but with about eight channels from which to choose. The reeds were six to eight feet high; so all in all, I had the usual pain in the arse dilemma. The main channel was pretty damn choppy and boily, but it looked doable so off I went.

An eddy is an area of re-circulating water behind an obstacle (usually a rock), and it allows you to break out of the current and have a breather. This gives you time to look ahead and make a plan. The more serious the water, the more important it is to have eddies. This next section didn't have any eddies to start with, and I just managed to hold it together till it started to get ugly. Luckily there was an eddy on the right just before the nasty bit, and I broke out of the main flow into the safety of the reeds. Clambering and dragging my canoe over numerous fish traps, I finally came across a right angle bend of rock. It was no more than fifteen metres wide with the whole river pulsating through it. It wasn't so much white water as hugely powerful rising and falling boils. As if on cue a teenager popped up and gesticulated that I needed to wait for the right time to paddle it, and when he realised I understood the message held up his hand and studied the water. Carrying the boat around would have been a lot safer, but instead I put on my buoyancy aid and waited for him to give me the go ahead. I put all my trust in this complete stranger with a friendly face. After about five minutes down went the hand frantically waving me on, and twenty-seconds later it was all over, job done. I gave him some fishhooks and line for that little gem.

I had been warned about hippos for months and hadn't seen one yet, but as the river started to widen, their tracks were becoming more common. It was only a matter of time. At least on the water they had somewhere to go, but on the bank it was a different ball game. You didn't need the expert skills of Ray Mears, or to share his uncanny resemblance to the creature to identify a hippo print, and sometimes the only bit of dry land around would be covered in them. On more than one occasion the dilemma then presented itself of where to risk going for a number two? Either precariously balanced on the end of my canoe, or at risk of a blubbery death in the middle of a Hippo trail.

That afternoon as I was paddling along daydreaming of chicken kiev, I was snapped out of my trance by the unmistakable shape and twitching ears of my first hippo of the trip. It was about ten metres in front of the canoe. Like all the others I saw on the trip, he was on his own. When they were alone, they were actually harder to spot. Sometimes I'd come across a fisherman just waiting there not doing anything, and as soon as he shook his head and waved his arms about you'd know why. Then you'd see the flapping ears and hear the unmistakable snorting. I used to get impatient and paddle around, but the locals would often sit there for ages. On this occasion there were no dramas.

Next up was the village and ferry of Kasongo, this was where I found myself being chased by the eight angry locals in two dugout canoes I mentioned in this book's preface.

They were just sitting around chatting when I initially came into view, and even though my Swahili was pretty good by then and I managed to explain myself pretty quickly, they rapidly became incensed.

All my instincts told me to get the hell out of there. Some of their faces were so screwed up in disgust, I did wonder what the hell I had done wrong. I know I'm from Essex, but you can't hold that against me. When a couple of them ran into the water to try to grab my canoe, shouting for money, I made the decision to flee. I didn't see any dugouts around, and the guys were clearly waiting for the ferry, so I didn't think they'd come after me. But after I headed off into the middle of the river with shouts of "Mazungu" coming from both banks, I heard the unmistakable sounds of paddles banging against the sides of a dugout. I then made a conscious effort to paddle as powerfully as possible, putting my whole body into every stroke.

I still had three thousand dollars in cash on me, along with my still camera and video, and I was damned if I was going to give them anything. I was pretty sure these guys were not bluffing and were prepared to get violent unless I put the fear of God into them. For me, if you threaten to fight, you've got to be prepared to fight. I even tried to visualise a machete battle to get myself mentally prepared for the worst-case scenario.

I didn't look around, hoping and praying they had given up the chase. Even my thick canvas top was soaked, and I could feel the sweat running down my body. Twenty minutes later, convinced they couldn't have kept up, I glanced around and to my horror there were still two dugout canoes with four guys standing up in each, paddling like madmen and less than twenty metres away. When they saw me stop, the shouting got louder: "Mazungu! Give us money!"

I've never started a fight in my life, but I've finished a couple. I knew that if the shit hit the fan, I needed to morph into a raging madman. And that's exactly what I did. I stood up, turned around and completely lost it, going absolutely crazy. Waving my machete around and shouting and screaming like a lunatic, I unleashed a torrent of abuse and threats at them, firstly in English then in French. I don't remember exactly what I said – suffice to say it wasn't complimentary. When I finally stopped frothing at the mouth, I noticed they were just standing there, motionless, with their jaws open.

Because they'd stopped paddling and their jaws had dropped, I knew it was all over, but I was still really angry and pissed off that they had driven me to lose my temper. There were a few more whimpers for money, but the fight had clearly drained out of them, and they didn't paddle any closer. I finally sat back down and paddled off. It took me a couple of hours to calm down, but I was also pleased with myself for not having backed down. If nothing else, the experience certainly gave me added confidence.

As sympathetic as I was to the plight of the Congolese people, this did not extend to allowing myself to be bullied or robbed. Intimidation of foreigners is rife in Central Africa, and only by standing up to people could you ever hope to change it. As I grumpily paddled off I was absolutely furious, both with myself for losing it and with the mob mentality of my pursuers.

I didn't know it at the time, but shortly after Kasongo there was a village of once great historical significance. Nyagwe was once an Arab slave trading town. The explorer Dr David Livingstone was the first white man to visit it back in 1871, while searching for the source of the Nile. He wanted to buy canoes to explore downriver to the North, but after building a house and staying for two and a half months, he failed to find anybody willing to sell him any. As this was as far into the forest the slave traders had penetrated, it's understandable that the locals didn't want foreigners to travel further into their domain. As Livingstone was the first white man they had seen, they probably didn't distinguish him from the Arabs.

After witnessing a massacre of some four hundred locals by the Arabs, apparently started whilst haggling over a fowl in the local market, Livingstone left in disgust, but wrote of the incident:

The open murder perpetrated on hundreds of unsuspecting women, fills me with unspeakable horror. I cannot think of going anywhere … I cannot stay here in agony … I see nothing for it but to go back to Ujiji.

In 1876, Henry Morton Stanley finally joined the Congo River here, having trekked overland from Zanzibar with the intention of following it north downstream to wherever it finished up. It would either turn out to be the Nile, flowing eventually into the Mediterranean, or the Congo into the Atlantic. (He wasn't sure at the time.) The other safer option was to head south into Katanga province, and to follow the Zambezi River to the sea, which in itself would represent a major feat of exploration. The cannibal tribes downstream were said to have been so fierce and warlike, and his chances so slim, he called his boatman Frank Pocock into his hut, and said to him:

Now Frank, my son, sit down. I am about to have a long and serious chat with you. Life and death – yours as well as mine, and those of all the expedition – hang on the decision I make tonight.

He then went on to explain all the dangers. How David Livingstone after fifteen thousand miles of travel, and a lifetime of experience in Africa, would not have given up his brave struggle to follow the river without strong reasons. Back in 1874, another explorer Verney Lovatt Cameron had also got as far as Nyagwe, but was unable to find canoes. He also heard fresh horror stories of what lay ahead on the river. Even though Cameron's party consisted of a hundred men, including forty-five askaris (soldiers) armed with snider rifles, he decided not to continue:

The tribes used poisoned arrows, a mere scratch from which proved fatal in four or five minutes, unless an antidote, known only by the natives, was immediately applied. And they were cannibals, more cruel and treacherous than any we had yet met.

Consequently stragglers would most certainly be cut off, killed and probably eaten.

A Kentish fisherman by trade, Frank Pocock in his discussions with Stanley, finally came up with an idea:

"I say, sir, let's toss up: best two out of three to decide it… Heads for the north and the Lualaba; tails for the south and Katanga."

Six times the rupee coin came up tails for the south, so he drew straws instead, but still he drew short straws for the south.

He finally threw the coin and the straws to the floor, and said:

"It's of no use Frank, we'll face our destiny despite the coin and the straws. With your help my dear fellow, I will follow the river north."

Stanley's plan was different from his predecessors. Instead of waiting to obtain canoes at Nyagwe, he decided to head overland through the forest until he could find canoes. They passed through many villages lined with human skulls, and with human bones scattered around cooking sites.

Day after day the caravan fought its way through the primeval forest:

We had a fearful time of it today ... such crawling, scrambling, tearing through the damp, dank jungles, and such height and depth of woods ... our expedition is no longer the compact column which was my pride. It is utterly demoralised ... It was so dark sometimes in the woods that I could not see the words which I pencilled in my notebook.

A couple of days later after I had calmed down, I arrived in Kibombo, the start of the last rapids section before Kindu, the halfway point of my trip. There must have been about fifteen dugout canoes all moored up close together under the shade of a large overhanging tree. Sitting on the roots also in the shade were a group of friendly guys chatting and watching the world go by. No shouting, no dramas, no demands for money; a very different story from Kasongo.

Somebody asked if I could wait while they fetched the immigration guy, and another even bought me some bananas and refused to let me pay for them. A few of the kids just sat there staring, but sitting in the shade chatting with a couple of old guys watching the river go by, I wondered what made some villages hostile and some so welcoming. Maybe it was just a question of the number of positive and negative people within a group, with the greater number influencing the rest.

After half an hour the immigration chap still hadn't turned up, and as a fisherman had offered to show me the safe way through the rapids I said my farewells and left. As it turned out the rapids from here to Kindu were nothing at all; a few ripples. At one point the immigration guy (complete with white shirt and black beret) was paddled out to meet me and asked for fifty dollars to fill out an immigration form. He knew that I knew it wasn't necessary, and reluctantly kept backing down asking for lower and lower sums. In the end, as he was such a nice bloke I gave him five dollars. I was breaking my own rules, but you'd have to have a heart of stone not to feel some sympathy for these people, especially the really polite ones.

★ ★ ★

The river here would alternate between wide and slow moving with the occasional hippo, to much faster with plenty of rocks. All in all easy paddling, and though I felt pretty rundown I was looking forward to getting to Kindu for a bit of a rest.

You know when you meet somebody, and all your senses tell you this person has got issues: well, a couple of days before Kindu, one such person came paddling out to say hello. In fact there were two guys, but laughing boy did all the talking. They were in separate dugouts and must have been in their late teens. The chatty one insisted that he guide me to Kindu, as there were dangerous rapids ahead. I didn't believe a word of it, and politely declined. But what this guy lacked in manners, he made up for in perseverance. Eventually he cut to the chase and arrogantly demanded that I gave him money.

"Donnez moi l'argent, monsieur," he said.

When I realised he might be trouble, in full view and to plant the seed of doubt in his mind, I moved my machete and placed it on my deck within easy reach.

"Donnez moi machete," he continued.

It seemed that virtually everybody I met asked for money. I had sympathy for those driven to desperation by poverty, but I was only human, and try as I might not to lose my temper, this teenager's incessant nagging was pushing all the wrong buttons inside me. He was like a stuck record.

Next up, he exchanged words with his mate and they started to bang into my canoe, effectively cutting me up, whilst still demanding money. At one point I rather forcefully pushed his dugout away with my paddle and he went crazy.

"Ah, you must pay for the repair!" he screamed, looking at his mate for support. "You have damaged my boat,"

'I'll damage you in a minute if you don't shut up,' I thought.

"What bleeding damage? You're an imbecile," I said trying and failing to think of the word for idiot in French. It was close enough.

"You cannot call me an imbecile," he said, enraged. "You have insulted me, you must pay me money for the repair."

"Please go away," I said calmly, and for the last time.

As a young boy, my hero was Grasshopper alias Kwai Chang Caine from the TV series *Kung Fu*. He never lost his temper, was very humble and quietly spoken, but when the bad guys struck the first blow, he could kick ass like no other. I remember once making a citizen's arrest on two scumbag skinheads who tried to steal my mountain bike. I rugby tackled them both through the entrance of a Body Shop, knocking over a towering display of shampoo bottles in the process. I then locked the doors behind me, before getting one of them in an arm lock, and fending off the other until the police arrived. The reason I'm telling you this, is that I like to think I have a sense of fair play. I probably would have been justified in landing some serious punches on these guys, but trying to emulate my boyhood hero, I didn't deem it necessary. In the end the police came and they were arrested.

Back on the Congo, I was again fighting hard to remain patient and not get carried away. The terrible twins had now cut across my front, and seemed to be closing in for the hard sell. The incessant "give me money, give me money, give me money" eventually pushed me over the edge. If I had been religious I may have said to myself "forgive them, for they know not what they do," but unfortunately for this character I was an atheist, so instead I stood up and took a deep breath.

"Shut the fuck up!" I shouted at the top of my voice. I then raised my paddle up high, and swung it at his head, stopping an inch from his scalp. It had the desired effect as he cowered and nearly fell out of his canoe.

"Now fuck off!" I screamed as our eyes met, jabbing my finger in his direction. He got the message and scarpered. I honestly think I lost my temper more on this expedition than I had done in the previous twenty years.

* * *

After Kongolo, Kindu was the biggest town so far, and I had heard it had a UN base so thought it must have a few luxuries. I couldn't help myself occasionally dreaming of a soft bed and a cold coke. It was a twelve-hour paddling day to get there, and I finally arrived just as it was getting dark and the mosquitoes were coming out to feed. On the plus side, it was too dark for anybody to recognise that I was a stranger in town. For some reason I felt especially drained, and I was keeping my fingers crossed nobody gave me any hassle on arrival.

Within a minute of landing, and before the crowds had a chance to gather, I found four local guys to carry my canoe to a guesthouse a few hundred metres away. Another minute and we agreed a price – but then the soldiers turned up, and my hopes for a peaceful, mosquito free reception faded.

"I am a marine," one announced proudly jabbing himself in the chest.

'So what?' I thought.

"You must come with us," he demanded.

"Tomorrow morning," I replied. "I'll come and see you tomorrow."

Since the crowd was getting bigger and noisier, pushing and shoving, I ordered my guys to get going – which they tried to do. But after five minutes of arguing, and when the soldier boys starting grabbing, I realised I may as well give in before it got ugly. "Okay, okay, but don't touch me," I said, knocking an arm away.

We were led to a walled enclosure in the dark, and I was given a chair by an oil lamp on the floor – at which point the officer turned up. I could feel myself being bitten, but was actually quite enjoying sitting in a chair with a back rest, looking up at the stars. The crowds had gone and I listened to the officer.

I do believe there's good and bad in all of us, usually expressed through patience, compassion, empathy and unselfishness on the one side, and impatience, cynicism, paranoia and anger on the other. Because the latter requires more energy, I found that whenever I was really, really tired (as I was now), I was generally at peace with the world.

I explained slowly and quietly to the officer: "I have been paddling for twelve hours, I have all the correct paperwork, there is no need for me to pay any money. I understand that your government does not pay you, but I have a long way to go and need my money. I would be happy to come back tomorrow but for now, I would like to go to my guesthouse."

He stood up, shook my hand and said: "That will be all."

Top bloke.

★ ★ ★

Once upon a time, Kindu must have been quite an important town. Surrounded by jungle, the river's edge was teeming with dugouts buying and selling all manner of goods from cane sugar to beer. Although the streets were lit with oil lamps, giving the place an ancient, spooky appearance, the substantial, albeit rundown, buildings suggested a one-time metropolis. We made our way up the dirt high street, canoe on our shoulders, and although the guesthouse had a fan, a toilet, shower, sink and a light bulb, none of which worked, at least there was a bed and it was secure.

I moved to a simpler, cheaper place the next day run by a

Moroccan guy, and walked the streets gorging myself on street cooked beef, barbecued over old oil drums.

My favourite place was like the McDonald's of Kindu, but the running costs were probably a lot less. Early every morning in the middle of town a single cow (when available) was slaughtered, butchered and wheel-barrowed off to be sold at various points. You could tell where the vendors were heading thanks to the trail of blood left behind. No part of the animal was wasted, and the guys doing the butchery, with blood up to their elbows, were true masters of their trade, even if a food hygiene inspector might have had a few words to say. They set up shop in their respective spots, and tried to get as much money as they could from the crowds of women who were trying to spend as little money as possible. The woman who ran my favourite spot, would then walk back to her oil drum with her paper parcel, get the fire going and chop up the meat into price sized pieces. Her restaurant was simple but effective. A bench and table surrounded by a cotton sheet hung from various points to help keep the dust out, and for a bit of privacy. The only other ingredients on the menu were little fist-sized balls of fufu and a potent chilli sauce. It wasn't the Ritz, but after what seemed like a lifetime of eating fish and rice, it was absolute luxury.

The local UN base was surrounded by razor wire fences and armed guards in watchtowers. Most locals thought the UN were a waste of time, however. Directly outside their compound was the best, most expensive store in town selling western luxuries like Pringles crisps and processed cheese for the privileged few. The only white faces I ever saw here were sitting in the back of air conditioned land cruisers, and as I would sometimes sit drinking tea from my other favourite street vendor (a colourfully dressed, very attractive smiling woman), you would see them pull up and stock up on tit bits.

★ ★ ★

I had a horrendous headache the next day, and felt as weak as a kitten, so I thought it might be a good idea to get a blood test. Sure enough it said I had malaria, and it was plasmodium falciparum the most dangerous variety. I also needed some Ciprofloxacin for my diarrhoea, so I took my prescription across the town to the pharmacy. As I was trying to explain I didn't want the malaria treatment as I already had my own, it all went black. I had passed out and collapsed unconscious.

Luckily I didn't die, and woke up on the floor with a small crowd around me. On my way down I had apparently smashed a pane of glass, and all I could remember was thinking, 'heartless bastard,' as the totally unconcerned shop owner serving another customer demanded that I pay twenty dollars for the damage. I've had malaria a couple of times before, both in West Africa, but I didn't remember feeling as bad as I did now. I actually felt as though my time was up. I couldn't stand up, I was struggling to stay conscious, and I was sweating like a mad thing. I also had the world's worst headache.

Eventually I regained the strength to sit on a chair, and after drinking a bottle of water, thanked the one guy who had helped me throughout. He also gave the shop owner a rollicking for not caring, and the price for the glass eventually came down to five dollars. I still felt terrible, and realised I had to get back to my room to take my malaria treatment, Riamet, which was supposed to be the best on the market. I could barely walk so I asked my new mate to get me a motorbike taxi. After a bumpy ten-minute ride with barely enough strength to hold on, I staggered into my room. I remember being so weak, I struggled for quite some time to get the lid off my medical kit, but incredibly, after six hours of taking the tablets I felt a bit better. After spending the next day in bed, I then felt strong enough to get back on the river the day after that. Probably not a good move in hindsight, but my obsession to make constant progress was strong.

★ ★ ★

It took me four long days to paddle to Ubundu; days that seemed to drag on forever. The water was horribly sluggish and the surrounding jungle was getting thicker, which, along with the increasingly hot sun, took a toll on my energy levels. I had at least nearly finished my malaria treatment, and hoped I'd seen the last of it.

A welcome distraction came in meeting a couple of lovely old fishermen on a particularly remote stretch Ubo and Maci were real characters, and had a great little fishing camp on a tiny island. Every experience they'd ever had was written on their faces. Their feet were cracked and leathery, their clothes were barely holding together, but they carried a great dignity and wisdom, which you'd rarely find in our so-called civilised western world. This is why I loved Africa, because it reminded me there's more to life than the eternal search for material wealth, comfort and security. Not that these guys wouldn't have given their right arm for a million quid – but you know what I mean.

They had metal hooks, but everything else they carried was made from the forest. The standard method of fishing in these parts was homemade jungle twine, with a floating stick on one end, and a rock with a length of twine and hook on the other. After they'd baited the hooks with a special paste, they'd paddle out into the river in the evening and drop them overboard at regular intervals, before checking them the next morning. In the morning I gave a T-shirt and hooks to Ubo and a reel of strong fishing line to Maci. I turned down the gift of a live tortoise, but then wished I hadn't, as a young lad turned up, blowing a trumpet of all things, and amused himself by holding a red hot coal from the fire to the tortoise's belly and shell. The poor thing would struggle to knock off the coal, before Miles Davis replaced it. I asked him to stop, but he just smiled. It reminded me of the year before on an expedition through the middle of Borneo. A local guy had caught a large turtle, turned it on its back, and proceeded to gut it alive.

In the end I changed my mind and took the tortoise with me, releasing it later in the forest, soppy old git that I am.

* * *

As I was so knackered the next day, I was hoping to find a nice quiet solitary bush camp. I'd usually be washed, changed, fire made and fed, ready for bed and a peaceful night within an hour of stopping. But come late afternoon it was village after village, and with some menacing looking rain clouds brewing, I pulled into a small settlement. I had a stinking cold and a fever by this stage, but it would have been rude not to meet the chief and explain myself. After a while of meeting and greeting, I finally started to set up my tarp. It was getting dark. I could have, and probably should have, slept in a hut, but in my fatigued state I just wanted to be alone. Since a wall of torrential rain was now slowly working its way upriver I frantically tried to finish my tarp and get my fire going before everything became soaked. The trouble was, about sixty people, mostly kids, had completely surrounded me watching my every move. When the rain hit they didn't go away, they just stood there staring. I was now freezing, and when my food was cooked, they were still standing there watching me eat, a lot of the kids laughing their heads off. When I needed a number two quite quickly afterwards, some of the little kids even came down to watch me do that. If I had felt great, I would have had a bit of a laugh with them before returning to a dry hut for a bit of a chat. But as it was I was physically and mentally exhausted. When I returned to my canoe and politely asked the chief to disperse the crowd, I felt myself welling up and my voice wavering. He got the message, and after a few words I was finally on my own.

* * *

I reached Ubundu, the place *The African Queen* was filmed back in 1951, with Katherine Hepburn and Humphrey Bogart.

There used to be a regular train service from Kisangani, but the track is now completely overgrown. The only way in was on the back of a motorbike, the road is so bad. Back in 1997 this road was also the scene of a terrible massacre of Hutu refugees fleeing Kisangani, where one hundred and sixty people were supposedly killed. I shuddered at the thought, often so obsessed with my trip I'd often forget the terrible atrocities of the past.

There are six sets of rapids between Ubundu and Kisangani culminating in Stanley Falls just upstream from Kisangani. I had no idea how challenging the rapids would be, so I thought a couple days rest in Ubundu wouldn't do any harm.

Of all the rundown towns, in all the world, Ubundu had the most romantic appeal. It took the biscuit for the sheer contrast between what it must have looked like in the fifties and sixties, and the decaying mess it was now.

Right on the water's edge was a rusted solid riverboat, the only moving part of which was the large steering wheel in a raised cabin overlooking the river. The local kids were always up there, cranking the wheel around, playing riverboat captain.

Slightly downstream was a large concrete dock, complete with two giant cranes also rusted solid, and judging by the amount of long grass growing out of the cracks in the concrete, it didn't now play a major role in Ubundu life. The town jail next door had been built so solidly, it was one of the few buildings still intact, and for that reason had become the main offices for the town's immigration staff, who were like pussy cats compared to the blood suckers I had met previously.

Then there were the bungalows built so beautifully and spaced so generously with their cobbled patios, verandas and substantial gardens, you couldn't help thinking back to what life here must have been like back in the sixties. Some of the buildings still had the original paintwork, soft blues and yellows, now barely recognisable, peeling and cracked. And the general layout of the buildings in the gentle undulating terrain was almost picture postcard perfect – or would have been if it hadn't been for the fact that they were all falling apart and in ruins. Having said that, most were being used as homes with the roofs patched up as well as possible, and with an exquisitely situated central pond full of ducks, it still looked like a very peaceful place indeed. Above all else it was quiet, almost spookily so.

★ ★ ★

The Catholic Mission was set back about a kilometre from the river, and gave a pretty good indication of how prosperous Ubundu once was. Surrounded by steaming jungle with faded, cracked red brick walls and floors, its previous grandeur was still hard to disguise. The church spire almost rose above the treetops, but you could see that hardly a penny had been spent on the place in probably thirty years. Even the graveyard had become almost completely enveloped by the jungle, and I only spotted the ancient headstones by chance. It made me think preventing the whole area being swallowed up by the forest must have been a full-time job.

They offered rooms and full board for five, ten or fifteen dollars a night depending on the quality of the room. I went for the ten-dollar option, which was luxury (with candle lighting and a working tap outside). Each night I'd eat around the table with Father Gregory and his understudy sidekick in the main building. I thought it was a little bit odd that they were drinking neat gin, before I realised it was in fact water in old gin bottles. It was a real treat to sit on a chair at a table and have a variety of food laid out in front of me, and to drink water that didn't taste of iodine. They asked for my views on African politics and the West, and each night after dinner we'd sit around his laptop and watch *Delta Force 4,* probably the worst film I have ever sat through. It was the only film he had.

As I had no idea of what the rapids would be like between here and Kisangani, I walked down to the river to pick the brains of some fisherman, and it was here that I met a guy called Janvier. Along with some others, he was shovelling gravel into a dugout. It turned out these guys were mostly fishermen trying to earn a few extra dollars, and within five minutes of asking questions a small crowd had gathered around, all offering their advice. Occasionally this would turn into a big argument and I'd get pushed to the back, with everybody trying to assert their authority and superior knowledge. It got a bit heated, but it soon became apparent that even if he wasn't much over five feet tall, Janvier rose above the rest when it came to commanding an audience; and what impressed me was the way he did it. I don't think he knew the river that much better than anybody else, but he clearly had a talent for diplomacy and was certainly not afraid of confrontation. The guys were speaking a combination of Swahili and Lingala and though I didn't understand what they were saying, I understood enough of the body language to tell that Janvier was a born public speaker. At the same time he was very respectful of other people's opinions; and for that reason he himself commanded real respect.

Inviting me to one side, Janvier raised his eyebrows, wrinkling his forehead in the process, creating a dignified look that I would come to know well in the future. It meant he was about to suggest something that he felt strongly about, and that I'd be wise to take on board. But of course it was up to me.

"Mr Philip," he paused waiting for my full attention. "Mr Philip, it is too dangerous for you to go alone." I'd heard that one before. "The way is very difficult, and there are some bad people there. I think you need four of us to show you the way, and help to carry your canoe around the dangerous rapids."

My cynical self might just been thinking that all they wanted was my money, but my more human side knew that without respect and trust, travelling can be a pretty boring and shallow experience.

It seemed that the more serious rapids were immediately below

Ubundu, and then at Stanley Falls just upstream from Kisangani. In between was apparently nothing to write home about. They offered to show me the best way around the first set, but insisted I would need to portage around one section, and they would be happy to help carry the canoe. It seemed like a good deal so we arranged a price to leave the next day. As Janvier was the only one who spoke French, he became spokesman and also offered to show me around the village that afternoon – at which point he asked if he could come all the way to Kisangani to visit his cousin, and help me navigate the river. As he was such a nice bloke, I agreed. Besides being good company, I thought he would fit quite nicely in the front of the canoe, and with double the paddling power we'd get there a lot quicker.

The main village was behind the rundown version, and consisted of the standard mud and straw huts. As Janvier showed me round, I questioned him about his life here.

"My father was a fisherman, and so I too was a fisherman. But it is hard to make money from fishing. Building roads across the river, we can earn two or three US dollars a day." There was no bitterness in his voice. "I speak French, Swahili, Lingala and Kikongo. I taught myself, and sometimes I get work as a translator."

He wasn't bragging. I liked him.

"Do you have any plans for the future?" I asked.

"There is no help from the government, but I am trying to start a small pharmacy business. I just need some money to buy medicine," he said looking hopeful.

"Is there no hospital here?" I asked. "There is a small clinic, but nothing is for free. If we are sick, we must pay for medicine, if you have no money... Maybe you die."

It transpired that he was also a pastor of his local church, which was not on the same scale as the Catholic mission but a much smaller Pentecostal denomination. He was married with one kid and another on the way.

Pretty soon after leaving Ubundu the next day, I saw the twisted steel wreck of an old paddle steamer that had been smashed on the rocks decades previously. You can imagine what it must have been like in the old days. With the strength of the current, especially during the monsoon, any engine failure however brief would cause you to get swept downstream very quickly indeed, with devastating results.

The river quickly became a labyrinth of channels once again, with the constant roar of a major rapid somewhere off in the distance. We seemed to be hugging the left hand bank, and after a few easy rapids the going became a little trickier. A few times I chose to paddle the rapids rather than portage, which the others were not very happy about, but after they saw my much lighter canoe dodge the rocks, and shoot the shoots, they were all cheering me on, and took on a newfound respect for my canoe.

The main portage was through an almost prehistoric bamboo forest. With little sunlight penetrating the thick canopy above, it was a spooky place to be and almost totally silent. I'd never seen bamboo as thick. Some of it was as wide as my waist, and interlaced with gruesome looking spiders webs you wouldn't want to stick your head in. Though it was frustrating not to see the rapid I was trying to avoid, everyone seemed pretty serious about it not being an option for me to paddle. After half an hour we were back on the main river, and my new friend Janvier and I said our farewells to the others.

Although it has to be said that Janvier was an incredibly confident person, he was never arrogant, and actually came across as quite a humble character. As we began to meet the odd fisherman on route, it also became clear he was a natural orator, with a million facial expressions to match. My favourite was his raised eyebrows and pursed lips look as if to say, "Is that right?' or, "Really?" But when he really came to life was after we arrived at a village for the night and every man, woman, child, dog and duck turned up to see what all the fuss was about. He absolutely loved it. Especially because most local fishermen didn't really speak French that well, and his Swahili and Lingala were excellent. He must have felt like the Pope such was everybody's willingness to hear what he had to say. They then would politely ask more questions about the Mazungu. After a while the kids would get bored and wander off, leaving the elders to discuss the finer points of the bible with him. Of course I'd have loved to take part in these discussions, but I don't think my atheist views would have gone down too well.

Our first night, pretty much panned out as above and after a couple of hours I fell asleep next to my canoe in the porch of the local pastor's house leaving Janvier to discuss theology. The next morning the heavens opened and I got a better look at the village from the comfort of the pastor's porch, which considering the whole house was built from mud and sticks with a grass roof, was pretty impressive.

A couple of things caught my eye. One was a guy hewing out the middle of his newly built dugout canoe with a traditional axe, seemingly oblivious to the torrential rain. It was about as heavy as you can get but it didn't seem to bother him at all. The other was the movements of a bedraggled looking chicken, running between bits of shelter. Anybody would have thought he'd never seen rain before.

Later on that morning when it was time to go, the pastor gave me the unfortunate looking creature as a parting gift and I tied it on the front of the canoe where it sat looking very pleased with itself. If only it knew what was going to happen half an hour later.

"Fish is not enough, you need meat also," the local pastor suggested. "You are my guest. We may be poor, but God tells me to look after you. I will bless you both for your journey ahead."

Janvier touched his heart and said something that sounded religious under his breath. I suddenly remembered the cheap watches I had bought as gifts, and quickly rummaged through my things.

"Please take this as my gift to you, I am grateful for your hospitality. You are a good man," I said as I handed him the watch. He absolutely loved it, but I couldn't help notice Janvier looked a bit jealous. The watch worked, but was like something you would find in a high quality Christmas cracker, covered in fake gold and diamonds. He quickly put it on his wrist and showed the crowd with cheers all around.

When it was time to go, there came the real highlight. With half of the village gathered around, we were blessed for the journey ahead by the pastor. Every now and then he'd raise his voice finishing with an "Amen", and the crowd would repeat it. I was actually quite touched. But then the singing started and I had to fight hard to stifle a smile. The words were in Swahili, but there was no doubting the tune. "Kum ba yah, my lord, kum ba yah", we all stood in a large circle and sang. Here was I, a confirmed non-believer, singing praise to God with what was, even if I say so myself, a pretty good bass baritone voice. I even began harmonising, which went down very well indeed. I felt like a bit of a harmonising hypocrite, but my intentions were honourable.

As confident as Janvier was in front of an audience, he was a nervous wreck on the front of my canoe. In one set of rapids during a meaty wave train, he leant the wrong way, held on for dear life and dragged us over. My first capsize of the trip, but my habit of tying everything in paid off, and apart from losing a few bananas it wasn't a big drama. The chicken got a bit of a shock mind you; I was surprised it didn't drown. The only real casualty was Janvier's Bible, which was pretty much ruined.

The only thing that drove me nuts about Janvier was his inability to produce a strong and consistent paddle stroke. Try as I might to teach him, he just didn't get it. After about four or five really powerful strokes, he'd paddle like a little girl for five minutes before having a rest for another five minutes (during which time he'd sing religious songs), before starting the process again. The real reason I asked him along was to help paddle, and although he was great company and a great guy, a paddling machine would have been nice. Then, stupidly, in demonstrating a power stroke to him, I broke my paddle in half. Luckily for Janvier, he got an easy ride the rest of the way to Kisangani, which was where I'd be able to fix the paddle properly.

★ ★ ★

After a couple of days we arrived at the Wagenia fisheries, just upstream from Stanley Falls and Kisangani. By the time Stanley reached here back in 1877, he had fought twenty-four pitched battles with river tribes, and after one particularly savage attack wrote:

We were being weeded out by units of twos and threes. There were not thirty men in the entire expedition that had not received a wound. To continue this fearful life was not possible. Some day we should lie down, and offer our throats like lambs to the cannibal butchers.

Then on another occasion:

The scouts retreated on the run, shouting as they approached, "Prepare, prepare! They are coming!" About fifty yards of ground outside our camp had been cleared, which was soon filled by hundreds of savages, who pressed upon us from all sides... We were at bay, and desperate not to die without fighting. Accordingly, at such close quarters the contest soon became terrific. Again and again the savages hurled themselves upon our stockade, launching spear after spear with deadly force... Sometimes the muzzles of our guns almost touched their breasts. The shrieks, cries, shouts of encouragement, the rallying volleys of the musketry, the booming war-horns, the yells and defiance of the combatants, the groans and screams of the women and children in the hospital camp, made together such a medley of hideous noises as can never be effaced from my memory.

Kisangani is the third largest city in DR Congo, and the furthest point you can travel on the river from Kinshasa before encountering rapids. It's surrounded by dense tropical rainforest. The only half-decent road to the outside world was built by the Chinese, and heads towards Goma, bordering Rwanda; but even this peters out into mud after a while.

The local fishermen must have thought all their Christmases had come at once when they saw me paddle up. Of course I would have to pay for permission to negotiate the falls, and obviously I would need a guide, which would not come cheap. Unfortunately for them I used to deliver washing machines and money was tight, even with the generous grant from the Winston Churchill Memorial Trust. Besides, the line through the falls was obvious to me, a sneaky little easy rapid around the main drop followed by pushing the canoe down the last bit on a rope. That was it. These guys weren't exactly starving; they were built like Mike Tyson, with muscles on top of muscles, and looked a lot healthier than I did.

I felt quite sorry for Janvier, however. On the one hand, his fellow countrymen were pleading with him to share the tourist's apparent wealth, and on the other, there was his loyalty to me.

Again it all got a bit heated at one stage, with some guy insisting I had to pay fifty dollars to pass. I wasn't having any of it and started taking the canoe down the route I wanted to go by myself. When I reached the main flow, which was pretty turbulent, Janvier didn't fancy it and ran down the bank instead, before jumping back in again in the calmer water below. Twenty minutes later I had the unpleasant task of navigating my way to shore through a minefield of human excrement, all shapes and sizes floating all around us, and continuing up the bank to the road. The sun going down didn't help.

★ ★ ★

I'd promised Janvier I'd treat us both to a slap up meal and a couple of beers on our first night in Kisangani, which is where he was due to be leaving me. After dragging the canoe through the streets and stashing it in the Hotel Kisangani (Janvier was staying with his cousin), it then took us over an hour walking around town to find somewhere that sold booze and a hot meal.

We ended up in a brothel unintentionally (honest), the only place with food and beer that we could find. The large bottles of Primus beer were ice cold and the stew hot. You might have argued that the girls were hot as well, but as attractive and friendly as they were, it has to be said that some of them looked pretty rundown and beat up. There must have been seven or eight scantily clad girls, mostly sitting and watching us eat. In the corner sat a monster of a guy with facial scars to match. I was dying to take the piss out of his yellow hat, but I didn't think now was the right time. Luckily he wasn't too offended that we were more interested in filling our bellies, than emptying our pockets on the womenfolk. All the while a rickety old fan chugged slowly along on the ceiling, looking like it might fall off at any moment. I just hoped the two cockroaches running along the floor, didn't find their way into my beef stew.

I spent five nights in Kisangani trying to regain my strength by eating and sleeping as much as possible. I ended up staying in the Christians' guesthouse Zongia, in the north of town. It was cheaper and cleaner than anywhere else and with food included. It cost me $10 a night to keep my canoe padlocked to a palm tree in the rather plush garden of the Kisangani hotel. The hotel was a dump but it was close to the river for when I eventually got back on.

I particularly enjoyed the street stalls at night selling various barbecued meats. After over three months of eating nothing but fish, I was beginning to look like one, and the opportunity to gorge myself on various meats was too much of a temptation.

It always made me laugh how much effort some people will go to avoiding local foods when travelling. I mean, what's the point in any real travel experience if you're not going to at least try new things, and to some degree experience how the locals live? Surely that's one reason for going in the first place? Yes, you will probably get some diarrhoea initially, but in going through this process you'll eventually develop a resistance to the point where you can eat everything in sight.

Pretty soon I had to make the decision whether to carry on, on my own, or to employ the services of Janvier again. Over a beer in the brothel, he confided in me that he would love to come with me to Mbadanka, and insisted that having him along would make life a lot easier for me with the locals. Mentally I was pretty exhausted. Physically my body would do what I goddamn told it to do, but I now had a thousand miles of flat water in front of me to Kinshasa and I needed to be realistic. As mentioned previously, Tim Butcher, the author of *Blood River* had got a ride on a UN motorboat from here. He then flew out of Mbandaka because he didn't feel well. As I was so tired, I have to admit to briefly entertaining the idea of buying an outboard engine, strapping it to the back of a dugout and doing the last bit as fast as possible. I quickly dismissed that as cheating, however; which it was. But the thought of having Janvier along did make a lot of sense though, especially as the next stretch had such a bad reputation for undesirables.

As there were no rapids, it wouldn't be a problem for him to sit at the front and in theory his presence would half the paddling time. To be honest, I had had enough at this point, and just wanted to get the trip over and done with; the interesting exploratory bit had been done upstream.

Decision made, Janvier would come as far as Lisala, and we'd think again from there, but not before I bought him the best quality Bible I could find, written in Swahili. It even came with its own case. I also bought him a sleeping mat and a few other bits, stocked up on rice, biscuits, nuts and bananas, some local malaria tablets, and after dragging the canoe down to the water's edge at dawn, we were off.

One of the best things about having him along was that he spoke fluent Lingala, which was now the common language. For months I had never been one hundred percent sure that people understood my Swahili – or vice-versa, but now he could translate everything into French for me. The trouble came however, when I didn't always want to hear what they had to say.

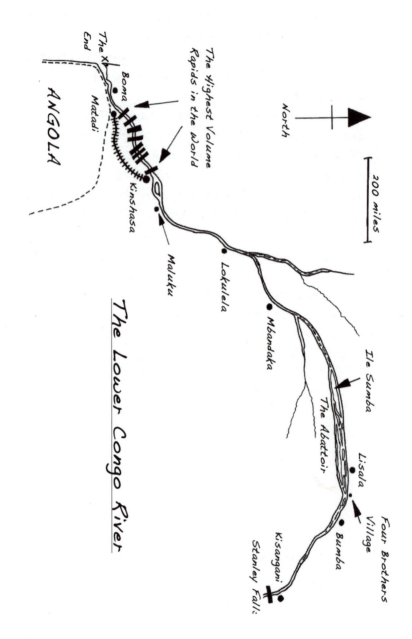

The Lower Congo River

ANGOLA

The X
End

The
End

Boma
Matadi
Kinshasa
Maluku
Lokulela
Mbandaka

The Highest Volume
Rapids in the World

North

200 miles

Ile Sumba
The Abattoir
Lisala
Four Brothers
Village
Bumba
Kisangani
Stanley Falls

150

THE LOWER LUALABA

Death Threats In The Abattoir

In *Heart of Darkness*, Joseph Conrad said that being on the lower Congo River was:

> *Like travelling back to the earliest beginnings of the world, when vegetation rioted on the earth and the big trees were kings. The air was warm, thick, heavy, sluggish. There was no joy in the brilliance of sunshine. On silvery banks hippos and alligators sunned themselves side by side. The broadening waters flow through a mob of wooded islands; you lost your way on the river as you would in a desert … this stillness of life did not in the least resemble a peace. It was the stillness of an implacable force brooding over an inscrutable intention. It looked at you with a vengeful aspect.*

A bit harsh, perhaps. "A vengeful aspect"? I don't think so, although I admit the climate on this stretch was particularly oppressive and debilitating, especially when I was directly under the full force of the sun all day. This heat, combined with an all too easily adopted paranoia and vivid imagination, could, I'm sure, result in an obsessive belief that everybody and everything is out to get you, it especially could have back in the old days when cannibalism was rife. I would often hear drums at night, but that didn't necessarily mean, "sharpen your knifes, there's a white man coming." It usually meant there was a party going on.

I don't think the Congolese people are particularly happy about the way their country has been portrayed by the West. Maybe the

Congo is not the most peaceable country in the world, and in places it's downright dangerous, but part of the blame for that has to go to the criminal exploitation of greedy western governments, and the unrest stirred up because of it. As Conrad himself described it:

"The vilest scramble for loot that ever disfigured the history of human conscience."

Within a few hours paddling on the first day out of Kisangani, Janvier was getting into a few heated arguments with passing locals. When I asked him what they were saying, I almost wished I hadn't. Basically, they were asking him why he hadn't slit my throat yet at night. And then they were saying that if he didn't want to do it, then he should tell them where we were camping and they would come and do it for him – and they would all share the money. It happened three times in the first day, at one point it even came from an old woman. In the three weeks it took to get to Kinshasa, this would become a regular occurrence.

One time I recognised the word 'Mbaye' (kill him) and lost my temper. I stood up, held my knife out, and made Janvier tell the guy to come over and try. Not clever, but hey I'm only human, and I was getting fed up with being threatened and intimidated. In reality I had turned into a Jekyll and Hyde character: humble, meek, and mild mannered most of the time, but able to turn into a raging lunatic at the drop of a hat.

Every man and his dog had been telling us that the stretch from Lisala to Mbandaka was too dangerous to paddle. This part of the river was over ten miles wide at times, with hundreds of islands. Incredibly wild and remote, it was supposed to be a haven for bandits, cut throats and brigands. Not too many years ago it was also known for its cannibalism. The Engombe tribe would paddle out to the passing barges at night, throw homemade gaffs onto the decks before dragging off their unfortunate victims sleeping on deck, drowning them and presumably cooking them in their pots.

Since being cooked in a pot tended to bring me out in a terrible rash, I had devised a cunning plan. I was going to lash my canoe to a large dugout, then paddle during the day and float with the current at night, sleeping and cooking in it, not touching land till Mbandaka. Brilliant. I'd also employ the services of a couple of locals, preferably multi-lingual, highly trained psychopathic killers, with a soft spot for Englishmen.

A day after leaving Bumba we were hit by a humungous rainstorm, and seeking shelter in the nearest tiny settlement we had the good fortune to meet 'the bruvvers'. As we all sat huddled under a thatched roof while the heavens opened and I handed around some cigarettes, it transpired that this whole dwelling was in fact one family, grand parents, parents, six sons and their wives and kids. After a bit of a chat, with Janvier explaining our intentions, four of the brothers offered to accompany us to Mbandaka. They reckoned we would need four, as it was a very dangerous area. An added bonus was that they had a shotgun, which I insisted they bring.

We ended up spending the night there, negotiating the price. The four brothers each asked for a thousand dollars and I ended up agreeing on eighty each. Oh and I'd buy the food. They reckoned it should take between six to ten days; I would also need to buy a permit and shells for the shotgun in Lisala. Their dugout also wasn't big enough, and Lisala was only a day away, so I planned to buy one for them there, the next morning. I hoped to sell this dugout in Mbandaka, and the brothers would have to get a barge back up stream. We sealed the deal by sitting around the fire eating yanvee, a fish delicacy and drinking homemade booze from giant clay pots.

The father was a real character and took great delight in dressing up for me in his traditional leopard skin hat, then demonstrating to me how he made roofing material and home spun rope from the forest. The snails there were enormous – about the size of your fist

– and he reckoned in ten minutes he could gather enough from the jungle to feed the whole family.

The next morning, everybody said their goodbyes, the father offered all his sons some advise about the journey the guys all gave their wives some money for food for the time they were away and off we set.

Though only five feet nothing, Janvier had finally turned into a proper paddling machine when he wanted to be. Along with yours truly he could really put the power on, and we didn't hang about. Even with the four brothers paddling standing up in their dugout, they struggled to keep up with us.

Leonardo was the only one of the brothers who had been to Mbandaka before, and this time he fancied carrying on to Kinshasa. Like the rest, there wasn't an ounce of fat on him and he could paddle all day. He was also the only one to speak French (the others only speaking Lingala), and there was a distinguished intelligent look on his face the others didn't seem to share. He was also the most laid back. And weirdly, his face was virtually identical to one of my best mates, Vern, who was originally from Belize. The main difference being Leonardo didn't speak with a Geordie accent.

Leonardo's big brother Valatay, although a gentle giant, was built like the proverbial brick outhouse, and had a round face with three main expressions. There was the confused look for when I was trying to tell a story, or when he realised I was in danger of getting my throat slit. A neutral look for when he was paddling for hour after hour in the zone. Then when we were all having a bit of a laugh, an incredibly happy childlike innocent look with a smile and a laugh that would light up anyone's day.

John was the miserable sod of the group, wearing an almost permanent scowl and giving me regular evil looks. He obviously didn't trust me an inch. After a couple of days however he'd start sneaking out the odd grin, but only at the end of the journey when he nearly cut off his finger and I bandaged it up, did he lighten up a bit.

Maurice must have been at the end of the queue when the muscle genes were handed out, which is probably why he didn't like taking off his top. Though as skinny as he was, he made up for it in the style department with a full-length bright yellow outfit probably visible from outer space. When I gave him a Manchester United woolly hat (which he never took off despite the intense heat, and even though the others mocked him) it completed his legendary status as the Congo's most well dressed man. He also loved singing whilst paddling, and would often give us a local song, probably used for generations to help keep everybody in unison.

★ ★ ★

It was getting dark when we got to Lisala, and we all arranged to meet up the next morning. The brothers went off to stay with friends, and after getting our papers checked by the local navy, Janvier and I ended up sleeping on the deck of a rusty old barge for the night. I was shown a guesthouse for a dollar a night, but to be honest it would have been more comfortable sleeping in a swamp. The barge was luxury in comparison. Janvier even arranged for a local woman to make us a fish and rice dinner, which she brought to us on deck in the dark. The mosies were pretty bad, but under a star filled sky with the security of a Naval post less than a hundred metres away, we had a great night's sleep.

'President Mobutu' (the ultimate dictator) was born in Lisala. For years I had imagined it to be an intimidating place, but as it turned out it was quite a happening little town. Most of the action was higher up on a hill overlooking the more rundown riverside. I hired a guy on a motorbike to take me up top, but soon jumped off the back and refused to go any further. A duck would have done a better job. I didn't even pay him he was so unsafe, which he didn't like very much.

I wanted to buy a canoe wide enough that we could all lay down comfortably and with high enough sides that we would remain dry and stable when the storms hit. The first one I saw, I was treated as a source of big bucks, but they soon realised I was no mug when I started sticking my knife in the hull, and slowly they got better and the prices came down. Eventually I found the one I wanted but the guy wouldn't go below three hundred dollars. It was perfect; no leaks, high sides, wide as hell and with wood that was sound throughout. I tried the 'no thanks' and walking away approach, hoping he'd change his mind, but he wasn't having any of it. I eventually gave in and bought myself a dugout. I was even given a bill of sale, signed by both parties and an independent police witness in case anyone thought I had stolen it.

While I was looking at canoes, a little boy followed me around playing with something in his hands. Only when I made my way back to my own canoe did he make it known that he had something for me. To my amazement he had made a little clay model of me, complete with shorts, baseball cap and big nose. He clearly had talent and it was very impressive. It made me wonder how much wasted talent there must be out here, potential Nobel peace prize winners and god knows who else, tied in to the basics of trying to stay alive with no effective government.

I then remembered I had some little toy cars that I had bought months before, and gave him a couple of those along with some fishhooks and line. He was absolutely chuffed to bits – as was I.

After stocking up with rice, fruit, cassava bread and some fish it was time to head off. As quite a crowd had gathered to see us off, I asked Maurice to assemble the shotgun in full view. I didn't want any unsavoury characters getting any ideas about following us.

Unlike the dugout canoes in Borneo, where only the bottom was carved from a tree trunk and the sides were built up with home made planks, the dugouts here were built entirely from one log. Most unique of all was the way they were paddled standing up, with a weird little body movement on the paddle recovery. Everybody did it, and only when I had a go myself did I begin to understand what it was all about. Basically the spear shaped paddles were made from hardwood and weighed a tonne, and I reckon the only way to paddle all day and not exhaust yourself was to keep your arms straight throughout, using a little body shudder to prevent bending your arms on the recovery.

The variety in dugouts throughout the trip was incredible. Right at the start on the Chambeshi you had tiny little canoes no more than eight feet long, pretty much just for crossing the river and maybe putting a few nets out. In the Bangweulu swamps they were fairly long and very narrow, for making headway through the tall grasses. Further down on the Luapula, especially amongst the rapid areas, the canoes resembled the modern day white-water canoes, short and stubby, with a well-pronounced rocker (a curved hull, turning up at each end like a banana). Then finally down below Kisangani, and in general on the long flat sections, they were massive, often forty foot long and up to four feet wide. This was probably the cheapest way of transporting large amounts of goods up and down river – easy on the way down, but not so straightforward on the way up. When fully loaded with sacks of various foodstuffs, they were packed in a way that enabled young guys to walk up and down the canoe, pushing off the river floor with long wooded poles as they worked their way back upstream. One guy would start at the front, put in his pole and push off before walking back down the entire length of the canoe still pushing off as he went, then when he got to the end, he'd simply walk back up and start again. When you had five guys all doing it at the same time, one after the other in an ever-continuing rhythm, with one guy right at the back steering, it looked very well organised, but hard work. To help with the finances, they would often have a couple of families hitching a ride at the back, sometimes with chickens and a couple of pigs. These journeys upstream could takes weeks, sometimes even months. Each night they would either sleep in the forest or stay in a village. And we complain when a bus comes a few minutes late.

After a couple of hours we stopped at the forest edge, and

Valatay and John jumped out up to their waists collecting some clay. For cooking in the canoe, the standard method was to pack in a circle of wet clay in the bottom of the canoe then put a metal charcoal burner on top of that, and hey presto, an instant kitchen. When the clay dried it would all lock into place, and any falling hot coals would then be prevented from burning into the wooden floor. The bruvvers would simply scoop water out of the river with their hand and drink it straight. Janvier and I filtered it through my T-shirt and added iodine. Occasionally we'd come across a clear water stream running into the main river and use that, but these were becoming less common further downstream.

By drifting at night with one guy awake at the back to stop us hitting any islands, we managed to cover about twenty to thirty miles during the eleven hours of darkness. The daily routine would usually consist of nuts and fruit for breakfast, we'd sometimes stop for a wash in the river around late morning, and during the afternoon we would start asking passing fishermen if they had any fish to sell. If the sun got too hot in the afternoon, some of the guys would take a bit of a siesta before cooking up dinner just before dark. Because Janvier took on the role of cook, it was a bloody holiday for me. All I did was to help out with the paddling, and at first they didn't even think I should be doing this. But when they realised I could keep going for hours, I'm sure they quite welcomed it, especially when we had a strong headwind. The only time they weren't too happy about it was when we were in a dangerous area and they thought I might attract attention from passers by. As my own canoe was dark green if I was lying down out of sight from the banks you couldn't really tell that there was anything was out of the ordinary there.

The next stretch was one of the most remote areas of the entire trip, and the least inhabited. It passed Île Sumba, a large elongated island in the middle of the Engombe tribal area. In 1989, two Belgians were hacked to death and eaten by members of the Engombe tribe ("gombe" means meat in Lingala). The area was known locally as the abattoir, and I must admit that part of me thought all of the warnings about this stretch must have been exaggerated. The first tiny village we stopped in to resupply was a bit of an eye opener; and it confirmed the reputation to some extent.

Have you ever met anybody with a scary, wild animal like intense look, like they've just undergone some relentless nightmare experience? Well, this village was full of characters like that. No sooner had we touched land did they descend on our humble craft for a look at the new meat. Within minutes we were surrounded, and one guy with the most intense look of all came really close and just sat and stared at me. I don't think I've ever been looked at like that before; he seemed to be studying every inch of me before finally settling on my face. Such unblinking scrutiny and intensity made me quite uncomfortable. I worried he was identifying my prime cuts of meat for future reference. Like a couple of the others, including an old woman, he only had one eye. This guy also had an ugly scar running down his cheek and neck. As an old woman came close and gave me a similar grilling. I thought, "doesn't anyone bloody well blink in this goddamn village?"

The brothers had positioned themselves around me like professional bodyguards, and actually seemed quite nervous, especially since Janvier had gone off to buy some fish and cassava bread. I made a mental note to make sure the shotgun was assembled and visible in future, not so much for security in the village but to hopefully stop people getting any ideas about following us downriver. I held out the palms of my hands and looked Scarface in his one eye.

"Is there a problem?" I asked.

Nothing.

Leonardo translated and Scarface smiled, shaking his head a little too slowly for my liking. Even then he still tried to climb into our canoe, reminding me of Gollum from *The Lord of the Rings* with his sloth like movements. Valatay cut him short, demonstrating a new angry look.

When Janvier returned with our supplies, I was not only glad to get the hell out of there, but also happy to have my own personal protection team.

Everyday we had fish and rice, fish and rice, fish and rice, and to be honest with you I didn't mind it. As I sit here now writing this in my kitchen at six in the morning, I realise I've had fish and rice for the last three nights. Old habits die hard.

The brothers however, rarely got the chance to eat meat. So when we noticed a large plump eagle sitting on a tree stump, it was too much for the guys to resist and out came the shotgun. For a minute I thought about saying no, but then realised this was a world away from western values and got my video out instead. As we paddled back upstream to keep the canoe steady, John took aim and pulled the trigger…Nothing. After three more attempts with a change of cartridges, we realised our trusty homemade weapon was actually scrap metal. Still, we could always use it as a club. As we paddled off, the luckiest eagle in the world looked on, oblivious to its good fortune.

We had been lucky with the rain. There were not many downpours and when they did hit we had been lucky enough to be near a village. But as we were now in one of the most remote areas of the lower river, and the monsoon season was quickly approaching, our luck ran out. The clouds had been building all afternoon with thunder and lightning on the horizon, and about an hour after dark, BOOM … we got hit big-time. Luckily the brothers had seen it all coming, and that afternoon they disappeared off into the forest and came back with a dozen six foot poles, and a coil of rattan (jungle vine). Twenty minutes later with the spare tarp I had bought, we had our own improvised shelter.

The wind was bad enough but the rain was something else, and even though we rammed the canoe through thick foliage to the shore, within minutes our makeshift tarp had been devastated and we were all soaked to the skin. The guys abandoned ship and disappeared into the jungle while I rebuilt the tarp and settled in for a night of misery. Apparently there are more electrical storms in the Congo than anywhere else in the world, and I was actually quite enjoying listening to the incredible thunder. I'm sure we've all got our thunder and lightning stories, but I don't remember ever seeing lightning start from the ground and fork upwards, then start from the left and go right, and vice-versa. I didn't get a wink of sleep that night. The rice got wet and needed drying in the sun for two days, both canoes had about a foot of water in the bottom, but finally the sun came up and the weather calmed down.

As we passed one village, a woman started shouting from the bank, asking whether we could give her daughter a lift downstream. When we paddled in to pick her up, and the mother laid eyes on me, she changed her mind. Apparently she didn't think it would be safe, and that there was a good chance we would be attacked, since I was a Mondele (which is Lingala for white man).

★ ★ ★

Janvier was a lot more worldly wise than the brothers. He was a modern Congolese, whereas the brothers were old school, born and raised in the forest. But they were no less honourable and decent because of it. They were fishermen and fathers first and foremost, living in a tiny community where the work was tough but honest. In hard times they would pull together and share what they had, and as simple as their life was, I found myself becoming increasingly envious and impressed by something that they had, and I didn't: contentment. Maybe I'm talking rubbish and they were miserable day in day out, but I don't think so.

With Janvier as interpreter, we had some greats chats during our time together, and as our mutual trust developed, so did the depth of the questions. After one particularly heated encounter with some passing locals asking why they hadn't cut my throat yet, John, who had hardly said a word the entire time, asked Janvier to translate a question for me.

"Why do you trust us not to kill you in your sleep?" he asked.

As soon as he asked it everybody stopped and looked at me for my response. I thought for moment before answering.

"I don't know. But when I first met you, something in your faces said to me I could trust you, you looked like good people."

After Janvier had translated my response, they all looked at each other and nodded. John said, "Merci," and smiled at me for the first time. Maurice started to sing. I later asked if they had thought about killing me, and John replied: "If we kill you, we will go to hell," and pointed downwards. Maybe the missionaries hadn't done such a bad job after all.

★ ★ ★

After five days and nights we finally arrived at the outskirts of Mbandaka, probably the fourth biggest city in the Congo. After stopping for a wash and change of clothes, we headed up to the main area where there was supposed to be a guesthouse right on the water's edge. There were in fact two; one twice the price of the other with its own waterside bar and cold beers, and the other with the river for a bathroom. The answer: sleep in the cheaper one, stash my canoe in the secure shed of the nicer one, and buy our merry band a couple of cold beers each. When I learned that it was the first cold beer that Valatay, John and Maurice had ever had, I couldn't help feeling a little bit guilty that I may have contributed to the corruption of their simple but happy life.

Within ten minutes the immigration official turned up demanding his pound of flesh. I bought him a beer and that was it. Despite his requests for paperwork and permits, I couldn't be doing with it. He got the message.

I paid off the brothers in local currency in my dingy little room, and asked Janvier to pass on my concern that they shouldn't spend too much of it in (what was for them) the big smoke. Within forty-eight hours, Leonardo had spent the lot on beer and women, but his brothers were more sensible and saved most of it, waiting for a boat to take them back upstream.

I also paid for a room for Janvier. The mosi-nets were full of holes, there were cockroaches all over the floor, the door was virtually hanging off, but when it was shut I was at peace, and could relax. Washing and defecating in the river was the norm for me anyway, so it was no great drama here. At least I could go into town and eat to my hearts content. Everybody went to the toilet in the river. Often there would be people collecting water, washing their clothes and defecating, all within a ten-metre stretch.

I thought I had got lucky at one point. I was in the riverside bar writing up my diary when a beautiful European woman walked in and sat a couple of tables away. It was all I could do to stop myself running over and giving her a big hug. But as she seemed quite interested in her book, I didn't want to scare her off and instead settled down to my diary.

Within half an hour the weather had changed and the mother of all storms started to brew just upriver. It was only early afternoon but the skies darkened to the point where you thought the world was going to end, then the thunder and lightning started. Sheet lightening was coming from all directions, and a wall of water (a squall) started to head towards us from upriver. The bar was open sided but with a substantial roof, and I couldn't wait until it hit. Dugouts on the river were frantically trying to get to the shore but were then enveloped and completely disappeared from sight into the maelstrom. A couple of minutes before it hit, the wind went crazy blowing anything that wasn't nailed down all over the place, and then BOOM it was upon us and you couldn't hear yourself speak. Even with a roof overhead we were still getting wet.

Just below us, an unfortunate fisherman who had just made it to the shore in time was having a nightmare trying to pull his canoe up the bank, the waves smashing his boat into another. Though everybody else had no problems about watching his plight unfold, being the knight in shining armour that I like to think I am, I instinctively ran down to help my fellow canoeist. I was soaked to the skin and covered in mud in seconds. After his canoe was safely up, we shook hands and I made my way back up to the bar and I couldn't help notice the woman looking over trying to catch my eye. In the back of my mind I was thinking, "After a few beers we'll be back in the luxury of her room making mad passionate love." A fling to remember or the start of a life long romance perhaps? When I snapped out of my wild imaginings, I made my move.

"Do you come here often?" I joked.

My English humour was lost on her. Her name was Monique from Belgium, working for Medecins Sans Frontières, and she did invite me out for a meal that night. Again my imagination ran amok, typical bloke that I am. To cut a long story short, as pleasant as the evening was I didn't get the vibe she wanted anything more than a friendly chat – and a very nice chat it was too. The owner of the restaurant was an expat Lebanese guy, and explained to me how

Mbandaka was the hub of the Congolese bush meat trade: every week traders would come down from Kinshasa to pick up hippo, crocodile and ape meat.

The next night one of the guys who worked at the guesthouse, asked me for two hundred US dollars to pay for drugs that had been prescribed to him for a motorbike accident a few weeks earlier. I examined his abdomen as best I could, but in the end only felt I could give him some strong painkillers. It hadn't been uncommon on the trip to get requests for help, and I had given most of my medical kit away by the time I arrived in Kinshasa, but I did feel a tinge of guilt for not paying for his drugs as he was clearly in some pain. A week later, further downriver I heard that he had died. The thought that I could have prevented a guy dying and didn't, hit home a little bit. But then – I suppose –we could all saves lives everyday by giving to charity if we wanted to, but most of us don't.

★ ★ ★

I had been told my dugout canoe would be easy to sell in Mbandaka, and after spending half an hour mopping and cleaning it out with a large crowd watching me, I had high hopes of making most of my money back. I had paid three hundred dollars for it, and hoped to get back at least half, but in the end I settled for a hundred.

Janvier wanted to come to Kinshasa to visit the home of his beloved Pentecost religion, and stay with a pastor he knew. Even though I had been missing the freedom of being alone, I enjoyed his company more by this stage and within an hour of selling the dugout we were paddling out of sight of Mbandaka. The first night couldn't have been more of a contrast. We slept in a tiny stilted hut hamlet, dominated by an enormous stilted church with a golden straw roof. It must have been four times the size of one of the local houses and in excellent condition overlooking the river. The toilet was also one of the best I had seen so far. It had been built entirely from the forest, and consisted of a floating pier surrounded on three sides by a bamboo lattice wall, allowing you to do your business straight into the slow moving water a few inches away with an awesome view.

There were no roads or tracks through the jungle here, yet we were given a large double foam mattress each to sleep on, complete with mosquito net. When it was time for dinner we were even given china plates with metal cutlery, throwing our fish bones down to the pigs below. The patriarch was a really nice old guy whose positive influence and high standards clearly had an effect on all those around him, including us. Not bad for a country with no public services of any kind. To end up like this guy and not bitter and twisted showed the real quality of the man. Even though I had terrible diarrhoea whilst staying here, this guy and his values left a real impression on me as we paddled off the next morning.

The heat was now as intense as I'd ever known and even Janvier seemed to be feeling it. It seemed to be coming at you from all directions; there was no respite whatsoever. Jumping into the river had virtually no effect, and only with a strong wind did you feel a few minutes of relief when wet. When we were out in the middle of the water my white skin was pretty much unrecognisable from the banks, and I took the opportunity to work on my tan, but anymore than an hour at a time and I'd be burnt to a crisp. I liked to paddle for an hour and a half without stopping then have a ten-minute rest, munching on a few peanuts. The cool early mornings and late afternoons were an absolute pleasure, especially when the 'sheep like' cumulous clouds dotted the sky.

The variety and colours of the flowers were astonishing as I passed through and around the multitude of islands and areas of swamp grass. I've never before seen reds like it in nature. A particular flower common in the swamps and grasslands was such a bright deep red; you could see clumps of it from almost a kilometre away.

The locals weren't too keen on paddling in the rain, preferring to shelter in the nearest village if at all possible. I, on the other hand, having an obsession with making progress, preferred to push on. A strong headwind was the only thing that seemed foolish to battle against, as you could totally exhaust yourself in an hour. I must admit at times to possessing a bit of a masochistic mindset in the earlier part of the trip, and getting some perverse pleasure out of paddling hard for ten hours straight without stopping. Blisters would form, pop and then form again. I could hardly get out of the canoe at the end of the day, but boy oh boy did my rice taste good.

Janvier, understandably, had a different mindset, and would always prefer to head for the forest even before the rain hit. The day after leaving the Ideal Home exhibition village, we found ourselves in the all too familiar position of being packed into a tiny hut whilst the heavens opened, with half the village keen to meet the Mondele. Conversation wasn't really on the cards because of the rain and thunder, so instead I passed around some cigarettes to the men who in turn shared some chunks of python meat with us. It must have been a big old snake, as the chunk we were all nibbling on was as wide as my thigh.

That night we ended up in a very spooky village indeed. It was getting dark as we arrived and there was a lurking white mist rolling down out of the forest to the waters edge. Along with a group of villagers simply standing and staring in silence gave it quite a sinister feel. They wouldn't even respond to Janvier's greetings and just stood there expressionless, cut in half by the mist, arms by their sides. Janvier asked if there was a problem, before one of the older guys walked a bit closer and started chatting. Basically they were scared, and had never had a white man in their village before. A couple of them spoke French, and after I made conversation for a bit they seemed to relax and we were invited up to the village. When we were settled in for the night outside the chief's hut, a vision of a woman came for a look at the Mondele and I just stopped what I was doing and stared. She was one of the most strikingly beautiful women I had ever seen. Her long hair had been combed back in a starburst effect away from her face, which accentuated her stunning features, perfect unblemished skin and a powerfully mesmerising look. Though dressed in rags, at over six feet tall she had the presence of an Amazonian goddess. She definitely had a face worthy of the front cover of Vogue magazine. I would have loved to take a picture, but unfortunately as was often the case, I didn't feel very comfortable photographing people unless I had built up some sort of rapport with them first. I felt it was often rude and disrespectful and ultimately exploitation. Call me an over sensitive old git, but if someone stuck a camera in my face I don't think I'd be too happy about it. I was so tempted to ask, but as I had just arrived I didn't think it would have been appropriate. Bang goes my career as an award winning photographer.

★ ★ ★

Probably the closest I came to ever attacking someone was when we approached the outskirts of the village of Lokulayla, and we noticed a guy screaming his head off from the bank. From his body language it was clear he was angry and wanted us to go ashore; a perfect reason to ignore him in my book. But when he sprinted back to his hut, grabbed his rifle and started aiming it at us, Janvier insisted we paddle in. We had a bit of an argument, but as I had never seen Janvier this scared before, I relented and in we went.

The closer we got, the more I didn't like it. For one thing the guy was wearing combat trousers, and he was also pacing up and down clearly agitated as hell. When we touched the shore he wouldn't come down to the water's edge, and seemed strangely scared. Janvier went up the bank to talk to him while I waited with the canoe. There was nobody else about apart from a rather nervous looking woman and child sitting in a large dugout. They seemed to be waiting for somebody.

As Janvier did his diplomatic best to calm down soldier boy, a couple of guys appeared on the scene and one of them was in a right old state. His clothes were torn and dirty, and his swollen face was covered in blood.

"What happened?" I asked, as his mate washed off the blood. They both looked at me as if to say, "What the hell do you think happened?"

The bloody faced guy tried to mumble something but winced in pain. I noticed his left eye was almost completely closed.

"This man wanted money but we have little. My brother refused and he was beaten to the ground," said the other guy.

"Who is he?" I asked.

"I don't know, but he is crazy. I think he has been drinking. You must be very careful."

They were also here for the first time from upriver, and it was his wife and kid in the dugout.

"Bullying bastard," I mumbled to myself as I strode off up the hill, just in time to find Janvier who was already on his way down with the man himself. He was about 6'1" and built like a tank, wearing army boots, camo trousers and a white vest. He was indeed a muscle bound bastard. His arms were adorned with the Congo version of tattoos I had seen many times before; instead of ink and needles, they simply used a sharp knife or razor blade to cut patterns in their skin. He spoke French and was carrying both a Belgian FN rifle and a permanent scowl.

I went into my routine, smiling and explaining myself; the content pretty much always the same. What I varied was the style of delivery depending on the situation: humble and happy for friendly fishermen, and initially humble, then boldly assertive with a mad glint in my eye for bullies and crooks. It didn't seem to be working with this dude.

"Passport!" he ordered as he nervously looked to see if I was carrying something. It later became apparent that he thought I was a mercenary, which explained his initial fear. His eyes were bloodshot red, and the more he realised I wasn't armed, the bolder he became.

"Passport!" he spat again, holding out his hand.

I didn't really want to give it to him. I was pretty sure he'd just put it in his pocket and demand money. I opened my passport up and showed him my visa, but this only made him angrier.

"Give me!" he reiterated slowly with contempt, looking me up and down as though I was something unpleasant he had just trodden in.

"No, you can see from there."

I persisted, holding it closer. He then turned on Janvier, and when he started jabbing him in the chest I realised he probably had no qualms about hitting him.

"This ain't good," I thought. I need to get him on my own where I can do some intimidating of my own.

"Okay," I relented. "Let's go up to your hut, just you and me." I gave Janvier a reassuring look, but he was shaking his head. I made sure I followed the guy up; I didn't want to be hit from behind. In the clearing in front of his mud hut was a solitary tree surrounded by cannabis plants, and under the tree was another unfortunate victim cowering in the shade. He also had a bloody face and was in a foetal position in the dust, clearly terrified.

"I am force navale," sneered the bully proudly.

'So fucking what?' I thought.

"I am the commander of this whole area, you must have my permission to pass through here," he added.

'You don't strike me as leadership material,' I thought.

"I don't have to give you money, I have a visa in my passport," I tried, but quickly guessed he wasn't interested in my attempts at diplomacy.

"Give me your passport."

The vein on his neck was at bursting point. If he had been a kettle, he would have been about to boil.

His contempt for me was indescribable, and was written all over his face: total disgust at my existence. I wasn't exactly his biggest fan either at this point. My gut feeling told me he could get violent at any second, so I eventually gave in and gave him my passport. He quickly read it upside down before putting it in his pocket. After ten minutes of negotiating, and with me slowly losing my patience, he gave it to me straight:

"Three thousand euros, and I'll give you it back," he said calmly – at which point I completely lost it. Again.

"Three thousand euros? You're having a fucking laugh you ignorant prick!" I screamed, jabbing my finger in his chest. "Give me my fucking passport back."

I was exhausted, I had been on the river over four months, and I hadn't backed down yet. I wasn't about to start now. It was probably just as well I screamed it all in English.

"I'll give you five dollars and that's it, take it or leave it," I said. Then, back into French: "If you don't take it I'll give you nothing."

About the same time as I noticed his bravado waver, I also noticed the breach block of his rifle was rusted solid, and a cunning plan popped into my head. If all else fails, I could put a chokehold on him, and hold on for dear life till he was unconscious (not dead). At one point whilst we were ranting at each other with our faces inches apart, I visualised putting the hold on him, and when he got close I felt myself involuntarily twitching, on the verge of springing into action.

"Your rifle won't work," I said glaring at him and pointing to the breach block. The look on his face told me he had lost his bravado. Ten minutes later and five dollars lighter, I was on my way.

Half an hour after that, we had rented a concrete hut on the rivers edge in the village of Lokulela.

★ ★ ★

Back in the 1880s, the missionary George Grenfell chose Lokulela as the ideal site for his initial mission. He was the first missionary to explore the lower Congo River, and his steamboat *Peace*, having been tested on the River Thames, was broken down into eight hundred packages and carried around the lower rapids from the coast by a thousand men. He had it assembled at Malebo Pool (modern day Kinshasa) and then spent almost twenty-five years exploring the lower Congo River and its tributaries. When he first arrived in Lokulela, he told the chief he had come bringing the "burning light of God" to the people. The chief responded with: "Do you mean to suggest we are all living in darkness?"

Even so, it's probably fair to say that cannibalism was quite common at this time. When Grenfell asked another chief if he had eaten human flesh, he answered: "Ah yes, and I wish I could eat everybody on earth." And when Grenfell visited the principal settlement of Bangala in 1888, the people were busy killing and cutting up captured slaves in preparation for a feast. The pathway into town was lined by hideous rows of skulls, and most of the people were decorated with necklaces of human teeth.

Towards the end of his time in the Congo, it transpired his work was having an effect on some of the local traditions. He wrote:

Just twenty years have elapsed since I first landed at the foot of this cliff and was driven off at the point of native spears. The reception this time was very different. The teacher and a little crowd of school children stood on the beach to welcome us.

Meanwhile, back on the banks of the river at Lokulela, the evening light was perfect, and I was down by the water's edge chatting to an old guy who had just been out fishing with a fearsome looking home made spear. It comprised of six metal rods, hammered out to produce razor sharp half arrow tips, which were then tied onto the end of a seven or eight foot wooden pole, and splayed apart into a circle. All the cordage had been home spun from forest materials, with a coil of extra cord and a loop for the wrist in case whatever monster had been speared pulled the weapon out of his hands. It was the perfect opportunity for a great photo, and I was just trying to get everything right when the immigration guy turned up and somebody announced his presence.

"The immigration man is here!"

"In a minute, I'm talking to this guy," I said. The light would be gone soon.

"No. The immigration man is waiting for you," they continued.

"Yeah, yeah," I murmured finally feeling comfortable about taking his picture after our little chat. Another thing I liked about Congolese fishermen was their strong handshake. I said my farewells to this gentleman, and returned to an altogether different being.

The immigration guy with mirror-lens sunglasses and Hawaiian shirt seemed more interested in listening to his radio than looking at my passport. He nonchalantly held the former to his ear and put my passport in his pocket, nodding his head to the music. Bloody cheek.

"Passport or radio. You decide," I growled.

My paranoia of falling at the last hurdle was causing me to be extra-specially short with anybody who gave me the slightest grief. He seemed rather nervous after that and was quickly on his way

A couple of days later, Janvier completely lost it with a guy who made some threats from his dugout, and told us he was a policeman. I'd never seen him this angry before, and afterwards he apologised for the behaviour of some of his fellow countrymen – but wouldn't tell me what this guy had said. I think the time he spent with me was a bit of an eye opener for him, with regard to the hostility inflicted on visiting foreigners. He was clearly very embarrassed on quite a few occasions – and this also highlighted what a great guy he was himself. I was lucky to have him as a travelling companion.

In the next village of Nkolo he insisted on finding the chief and complaining about the guy who had annoyed him, who it transpired was a policeman, albeit a crooked one. Nothing new there then.

Apart from the bent copper, the rest of the village hierarchy turned out to be wonderfully welcoming. The village secretary insisted we set up camp in her garden just around the headland. The only trouble was that to get there we would need to paddle right out into the middle of the river before paddling back to shore, as there were powerful rapids right off the headland.

After what I'd been through upstream it all looked pretty simple to me, but I promised them I'd be careful. It was simply a rather powerful, boily eddy line, and even though Janvier was pleading with me to paddle around, I assured him it would be okay. The most important thing is to lean the canoe into the eddy as you cross the eddy line – and though it was a bit wobbly due to Janvier sitting bolt upright (I couldn't think of the French word for lean), we managed it okay. We then heard the cheers from the bank from the relieved villagers.

The chief visited us later that night. He was now in his seventies, but he told us I was the first white man and tourist they had ever had. Only back in the sixties had he seen white mercenaries pass by on the river. He also told us of a large group of rafts that passed by but didn't stop back in the seventies. I told him this must have been the Blashford Snell army expedition back in 1974. I gave him my compass as a parting gift.

* * *

There were definitely more armed locals than ever before as we neared Kinshasa, and by this stage I just wanted to get the trip over and done with. It had now taken over four months and I was terrified that I might fall at the last hurdle. I couldn't quite believe that I hadn't had anything stolen. I hope that doesn't come across as insulting to the African people, but I have experienced quite a few incidents of theft over the years, East Africa being the worst. I've had money ripped out of my hands, stereos ripped out of my vehicle, rucksacks stolen: you name it. In Cape Town I even had somebody come into my tent in the middle of the night and steal my wallet. I actually woke up as he was in there and ended up chasing him down the street stark naked at two in the morning.

The grief in the Congo however, largely comes in the form of intimidation and threats. It's not a place for the faint hearted, which is probably why I had become rather aggressive.

I don't know if you could buy immigration uniforms at the local markets, but the day after Nkolo, I did wonder about the legitimacy of some so-called officials. We were in the middle of nowhere, paddling along, not doing anybody any harm, when more shouts came from the bank. About four guys were running along the water's edge shouting for us to paddle in. There was no village for miles and only a solitary hut a bit further downstream. Janvier said we should go in, but I insisted it wasn't necessary – until a guy emerged out of the hut with a rifle and aimed it at us.

"C'est necessaire, c'est necessaire," Janvier screamed as I steered us into the shore. The guy with the gun then quickly went into his hut, before emerging a few moments later dressed in the white shirt and black beret of the immigration service. Lots of shouting for my passport followed. He refused to shake my hand, and I refused to take no for an answer, holding my hand out, like a lemon.

"No shake hands, no passport," I said, thinking a bit of common courtesy is what's needed here.

Eventually he relented and shook my hand – at which point I gave him my passport. He had an honest, intelligent face, and after he inspected my papers and I explained my journey he eventually offered another handshake and bade us farewell. A couple of his cronies didn't seem too happy he hadn't asked for any money, and suggested as much, but he had made up his mind and even gave us a smile as he waved us goodbye. A good handshake speaks all languages.

★ ★ ★

I was almost there. Just after the larger village of Bolobo, the multitude of islands had become a thing of the past, and the river now narrowed considerably picking up speed for the final hundred and fifty miles to Kinshasa. Lots of locals had advised me that corrupt officials and soldiers were a big problem on this stretch, constantly harassing even locals for money. I had become a bit blasé about the constant warnings and took them with a pinch of salt most of the time. I was now approaching the capital city however; a completely different animal to the wilderness experience and its usually humble, respectful indigenous population.

Apparently the last bit from Maluku through the enormous Malebo pool was the worst. For now I chose to use the cover of darkness to paddle through the night, tying my canoe to a dugout heading in the same direction. Due to the extra speed of the water, we managed to cover over a hundred miles in two days. This included a night on the water and considering the headwinds were an absolute nightmare, wasn't bad going.

Maluku turned out to be an absolute dump. As we paddled up to the ramshackle pontoon pier, all manner of unpleasant looking characters descended on us to demand money, offer their services and generally take the piss. I didn't have to speak Lingala to understand that Janvier was getting a real hard time. Occasionally everybody would burst out laughing at some insult thrown Janvier's way – and if he hadn't been so outnumbered he would have given as good as he got.

In the end I stood up and made an announcement: "This is my brother Janvier." I paused for effect. "The best man here."

I tried to make as much eye contact as possible, using my finger to emphasise that this statement included them. At least that's what I thought I said. Judging by their angry glares however, I probably insulted their mothers or something. Time to quickly move on.

In the end we decided to land somewhere else and paddled off. A bit further downstream we were fortunate enough to meet a schoolteacher who agreed to put us up in his concrete, windowless hut just before the rain hit.

I had been weighing up in my mind for some time, whether I should paddle into an area known as 'the beach' in the centre of Kinshasa or not. It was the main landing area for boats crossing to and from Brazzaville in DR Congo, and had a bit of a reputation as a wild, crazy old place, especially for foreigners. On the one hand I didn't want to fall at the last hurdle, and on the other I didn't want to bottle out. I was also intrigued to see how wild it was – and actually relished the challenge of getting amongst it. Surely it couldn't be as bad as they all said?

There was actually a pretty good road from here to Kinshasa and it would only take forty-five minutes by car. But as tempting as it was, I hadn't come all this way to start slacking now. Malebo Pool might have a reputation for the criminal element, but if I took precautions I reckoned I could still do it by river.

Formerly known as Stanley Pool, Malebo Pool is approximately twenty-two miles long and fourteen miles wide, with Bamu Island situated in the middle. It's a kind of no-man's land opposite

Brazzaville and that's probably the reason it has a bit of a reputation for criminal activity. In the end, I decided to hire a dugout canoe with an outboard engine on the back, which was wide enough to fit my canoe inside and keep it invisible from the outside. I then laid down inside, also invisible and chilled out as we set off on the hour-long journey. Because I'd spent a few hours of bartering the price down, it was late morning by the time we set off.

Some of the makeshift villages on the shifting sand islands were as poor and desperate as any I'd ever seen. At first glance they looked like windblown rubbish tips. But on closer inspection you could just about make out that virtually every piece of rubbish, had in fact been ingeniously used to build a multitude of huts of varying shapes and sizes. Anything rigid had been dug into the sand, and used as supports to string together pieces of cloth, or plastic, as coverings to keep out the sun, wind and rain. It was a patchwork quilt village in no-man's land.

At one point I stood up to stretch my legs, and within minutes, a powerful speedboat full of dodgy looking soldiers turned up out of nowhere and came alongside. At least they weren't shouting, which was a bonus. I didn't want to appear like a sheep, so I stood up and asked who the 'chief' was. I offered my hand to the young boss and gave him a handshake that nearly pulled him out of his boat. I didn't want to take any shit off these guys. After showing him my passport, I noticed one of them in conversation with my man at the back whilst handing him something. The cheeky little sod then pulled off our outboard fuel line and started draining petrol into his container.

"Oy!" I shouted. "What the hell do you think you're doing? Put that back!"

To my amazement, he did, holding his hands up saying, "Okay, okay."

They could have easily robbed us blind, but for some reason they were nice as pie – most uncharacteristic, or maybe I had begun to tar all soldiers with the same brush.

The skyline of Kinshasa had been visible for quite a while now. More rusting barges littered the shore, along with overgrown, abandoned roofless warehouses. I don't think I have ever seen so much rusting metal, and wondered how much money could be made if there was a means of melting it all down. As we drew closer however, the decaying past gave way to a less decrepit workable future, with functioning ports – albeit in a rundown state. Most of the boats were also homes to either crew or squatters. Some of them were throwing their waste into the river, which reminded me of something I had seen once before while driving through Mozambique. We had stopped for a break on the riverbank below a large bridge, and somebody on top threw a cloth bag into the water. I heard something coming from the bag, but only when it hit the water was I sure it must have been puppies. You could hear the yelps and see the bag wriggling as it slowly sank below the surface. To this day I still feel guilty that I didn't swim out to get it.

KINSHASA

The Atlantic Ocean or Bust

I imagined 'the beach' to be an actual beach, but it turned out to be a concrete, heavily gated immigration centre. Every now and then a large ferryboat would arrive from Brazzaville, with hoards of easy prey for the officials. I had seen this before on many borders in Africa, where the officials would stand watching the crowds for anybody who looked scared. This usually indicated that it was their first time across, and that they didn't really know what the procedure was. It also meant they would be more likely to cough up some cash if intimidated sufficiently. It was most often a young family with the mother holding a child, and the nervous father, his eyes darting in all directions attracting the attention of the experienced hawks who were waiting to swoop.

I remembered the first time I crossed the border into Nigeria many years ago. Our medical kit had been searched, and when they found our needles we were accused of being drug runners and ordered to pay a fine. We knew they were trying it on and simply refused. We were then made to wait outside on a bench till we changed our minds. Shortly after this a large truck clanked across the border with all manner of people hanging off the sides. You could see the bullyboy officials looking at us, and them and devising a plan, before screaming at the people to get down from the truck. Then out came the rubber hoses and they started laying into the men and women with impunity. Not for long, but long enough to strike fear into everybody, including us. Unfortunately for the customs men, we were on a tight budget and wouldn't give in – but the episode demonstrated the barbaric unscrupulous nature of some officials.

I didn't want to land directly onto the pontoon landing stage for fear of attracting too much attention, so instead we got out a hundred metres upstream. I had hoped we wouldn't be spotted, but within five minutes of landing, familiar shouts of "Mondele" were echoing along the riverbank.

The area we landed in must have been a public toilet, as there were little piles of individual expression everywhere you looked. Even the steady stream of police and officials were having trouble navigating the minefield of unpleasantness. It actually worked in our favour, as many of them wouldn't brave the final few metres down to our canoe – and that gave us some breathing space.

"Come here, give me your passport," they commanded.

"Not here, and not without my canoe," I replied.

So it went on for a while. In the end some of them helped us with the canoe through the minefield up into the main compound, where I insisted my canoe be dragged right into the corridor of the office complex. They started with the good cop, bad cop routine, then in the end they all sat around, cramped into a small office and listened with growing respect and nodding heads about my journey. There then followed a good-natured but heated discussion about whether my journey was indeed possible, and slowly but surely they seemed to come to a conclusion. One by one they got up to leave, shaking my hand.

Janvier was getting an equal grilling out in the corridor with the canoe. Though when we first arrived he had gotten a fair amount of grief, he had now gained a lot more respect, and he seemed to be quite enjoying telling stories about our time together.

After two hours without paying a penny, it was time to find a hotel and I insisted with respect that it was time for us to leave. Surprisingly they agreed and even supplied us with our own police bodyguard to help us find some transport. Even though everybody thought I was stinking rich, I was actually going to finish the trip three thousand pounds in debt (despite my grant), so I didn't want to splash out any more money than I had to.

While the police guy tried to find us a vehicle, I noticed there were loads of guys with barrows milling about looking for work. It seemed the cheapest option. Because we were now surrounded by a mob of fifty people, I quickly tied the canoe on an old guy's contraption and off we went. He didn't argue. It basically consisted of a car axle and wheels, with a metal pipe open basket welded onto it. It was then designed in the same way as an old-fashioned horse trap, but with a guy pulling it instead of a horse. When we had cleared the crowds I stopped and arranged a price.

Kinshasa (formerly Leopoldville) is a crazy old place, and is actually the most populous Francophone city in the world, almost exceeding Paris and Montreal combined. It was much like any other Central African city, but bigger and with worse roads. We must have been an odd sight, trudging off through the streets with a bloody great canoe sticking out like a sore thumb. It was hard to gauge the age of the guy pulling the barrow; he could have been anything between twenty and fifty. He was bare footed and dressed in rags, but there wasn't an ounce of fat on him and he was built like a gladiator in his prime. I tried to help him by pushing the barrow but this only upset the balance, so in the end I left him to it. I felt great though, as this was it, the trip was almost over. I dread to think how much I weighed, but the thought of a slap up fried chicken dinner was driving me on.

I so wanted to stay at the Hotel Estoril nearest the train station, it was luxury, but at eighty dollars a night wasn't justifiable in my books. So half an hour later, soaked in sweat we arrived at the secure Guesthouse Hotel at twenty bucks a night, at least it had a fan and clean white sheets.

Janvier already had some accommodation arranged at a church god knows where. It felt quite awkward paying him off and saying our goodbyes, but he seemed pretty happy. I had bought him a mobile phone and gave him a fifty-dollar tip.

"I wont forget you Janvier. You are a good guy. Thank you so much for your help," I said. I felt so lucky to have met him.

We stood on the street looking for a cab.

"No. I thank you Mr.Philip. Now I can start my pharmacy with the money you have given me."

"How long will it take you to get back to Kisangani?" I asked.

"Maybe one month if I take the fast boat... Maybe longer."

I worried that maybe I should have paid for his flight to Kisangani.

"Please be very careful with your money, Kinshasa is a dangerous place. Strap it to your leg. You must hide it somehow," I said. It was his first time in the big city. I wouldn't be able to bear it if he was robbed.

"Mr.Philip," he looked at me with his raised eyebrows, crinkled forehead look and took a deep breath. "I am sorry for some people in my country, we are not all bad. We have nothing, we have no help, so... Some people have lost God."

"I know. If there were more people like you, this would be the strongest country in Africa. You are one in a million."

I meant every word. We shook hands one last time. He had been a great companion, but as I paid his taxi fare and waved goodbye, I must admit it felt great to be totally independent again. I watched his taxi disappear into the night, and felt privileged to have met him.

★ ★ ★

There was no hot water in my room and some pretty big spiders were on the walls, but after sitting on the floor in the shower scrubbing myself clean for half an hour it was time to get some serious food down my neck. After a five-minute taxi ride I was sitting in 'Hunga Busta Chicken', gorging myself on the best fried-chicken Kinshasa had to offer. I had three pieces of chicken and chips times three, followed by a burger and chips, an ice cream and

183

four cans of coke. I believe I'd earned it.

Paddling through the intense heat of the day for months, I had been planning the perfect night out in Kinshasa: the best steak restaurant in town, copious amounts of cold beer followed by some live music, dancing with a Naomi Campbell look alike and hopefully a night of passion to round it all off. In the end I went to bed with a belly full of fried chicken instead.

Reaching the sea had now become my whole world, and despite the pleasures to be had in the big smoke, I decided to have only one full day off. The longest street in Kinshasa was the Boulevard du 30 Juin, signifying the date of the Congo's independence back in 1960. Some call it the Champs-Elysées of Africa. I walked the length of it to try and find the National Tourist Office, but in the end it didn't exist. Virtually every shop of significance had its own personal armed security guard, usually brandishing a pump action shotgun.

I decided to head off into the backs streets for a look at the real Kinshasa, and after only a ten minute walk found myself in an altogether different sort of street. Instead of the paved road I'd seen elsewhere in the city, the surface here was a dark earthy mud, churned up by passing trucks with large puddles formed in the tracks. For some reason the road sweepers and refuse collectors of the Boulevard du 30 Juin didn't venture into this area, leaving large piles of rubbish either being blown in all directions or burning. A pungent mist was left hanging in the air. Abandoned vehicles had become playthings for the kids. Mangy flea bitten dogs and the odd pig snuffled for food in the gutters. Then down the middle of the road came a guy in a three-piece suit with a mobile phone clamped to his ear, trying not to get his shoes dirty. Bizarre.

The South African guy I had met in Kongolo, although a massive fan of the nightlife in Kinshasa, told me he had been snatched by the police on a couple of occasions whilst walking around town here. A car simply pulled alongside him, and he was dragged inside before being driven around town and generally threatened and harassed for money until he relented. Now he only ever got taxis anywhere.

At one point, when in a taxi, I passed the Stadium Des Martyrs in the middle of town. It reminded me of the 'Rumble In The Jungle' – Mohammed Ali's famous fight against George Foreman back in 1974. President Mobutu had been so keen to impress the international community, he'd ordered his police force to round up one thousand of the most notorious criminals in Kinshasa and take them to the Stadium Des Martyrs. He then randomly selected a hundred people and had them shot dead on the spot, before warning the rest that the same fate would befall them if they caused any trouble for the duration of the fight. It was in the film made about the fight, that I learned the word "Mbaye" (Lingala for kill him), chanted by the fans of Mohammed Ali as he went for his morning run. This was how I'd recognised the term used months before, when the locals threatened to cut my throat.

The taxi drivers here were a little more aggressive than in rural England. My golden rule was never get in until a price was agreed (unless being chased by an angry mob). If you did, they had you by the short and curlies. I always tried to ask at least three locals what a ride across town should cost, and if they were not the same then I keep asking until I get an average figure. Then, when I hailed down a cab, I simply stated or confirmed the price as a matter of fact. The price here for a shared taxi ride into town was five hundred C.F.A (one dollar).

* * *

As much as I wanted to paddle the river from Kinshasa to Matadi, it would have been suicide to attempt it in an open canoe, alone. The rapids here are said to be the highest volume rapids in the world, with thirty-two cataracts over a hundred-mile stretch, and with whirlpools big enough to swallow a bus. The river here possesses as much power as all the rivers and falls in the United

States combined. It wasn't really an option for little old me on my lonesome. Maybe I'd come back and do it in the future with a team of rafters.

The cheapest way to get to Matadi was to hitch, the second cheapest was a bus. Paddling it would have been the most expensive option, costing me my life.

I first had to get to the Matadi Road on the other side of town. The hotel receptionist suggested the hotel gardener had a cousin with a friend who owned a van. After haggling over the price I was dropped off the next day at six-thirty in the morning on the Matadi Road. It was absolutely manic, and if any passing traffic could have seen me with my thumb out through the mob that surrounded me, maybe I might have got a lift. A very friendly express bus driver told me I could put my canoe on his roof for an extra five dollars. It seemed the best option. All I had to do then was wait for the bus to fill up.

After we tied the canoe on the roof, the crowd soon got bored and wandered off leaving me in peace to sit and observe Kinshasa life. The street was already a thriving mass of people, with all manner of vehicles loading and unloading their goods. As African buses go, this one seemed fairly well maintained. Down by the back wheels there was a woman selling chickens with their feet tied together. Occasionally they would jump out of her basket and risk getting trampled by passers by. A small boy leant on another wheel retching up a bright yellow fluid, while nearby a mother took down her son's trousers and let him piss on the floor right in the middle of the path. A tough looking young guy walked past, his face and arms covered in scars with a pair of pink women's knickers on his head. Nobody batted an eyelid to any of it.

As the driver insisted I sit up front, I gave him some money to buy a coke. Instead he sent his sidekick off with the money who then came back with a little bottle of forty-five percent proof whisky. Before I could work out in French how to say, "I hope you're not going to drink that now," he downed over half of it.

186

Then I stepped in and took it off him.

"I'll give it back when (if) we get to Matadi," I said and he made an instant sulking face.

When every last inch of space had been filled and I thought we'd be leaving, a guy got in the back with his good book and turned to face his captive audience. He then began a twenty-minute sermon with as much passion and verve as he could muster. There were plenty of "amens" – and plenty of bullshit from where I was sitting. Then just, when I thought he had finished, he started singing, and most of the bus joined in. The praying I was doing was of a different variety, but I felt justified in my cynicism when he finally passed his hat around asking for money. I don't think it was for his church. Probably half of the bus gave something.

As we left Kinshasa the rolling hilly landscape was a barren wasteland. Any vegetation of use had been stripped bare or ripped out of the ground. After a while, the whisky started taking effect and the driver began giggling like a school kid. The guy sitting next to me in the front, who had been screaming at the top of his voice into his mobile phone so loud for ten minutes that I literally had to put my fingers in my ears then began a never-ending series of requests to the driver for the rest of his whisky. It was like a classic "are we nearly there yet... no... are we there yet...no" stuck record. Only when we finally pulled into Matadi did the noise relent.

One of the women on board then suggested she come to my hotel room that night. Even though I said no thanks, she still knocked on my door a couple of hours later dressed entirely in tight white Lycra, dripping in fake gold jewellery. I can't say I wasn't tempted, and we had a nice chat, but I finally decided to decline her voluptuous offers in favour of the moral high ground and a good night's kip.

★ ★ ★

The next morning I dragged my canoe through a market and a rubbish tip and lowered it on a rope down a steep slope into the river. I was finally on the last leg of my journey and I reckoned it would take four days tops to the Atlantic. The last set of rapids, were half a mile upstream but, with steep rocky hills either side, the river here was still uncomfortably boily. No fishermen, no ships, I had the river all to myself.

Back in 1877, when Henry Morton Stanley was attempting to descend the lower rapids (now from Kinshasa to Matadi), the surrounding hills were heavily forested, making any portaging extremely difficult. His collapsible boats were made of wood and canvas and had been built in England, but he also had numerous dugout canoes taken as prizes from the warring tribes back upriver A local Chieftain, Itsi of Ntamo, told him there were three cataracts after Malebo Pool, the Child, the Mother, and the Father. We now know there are thirty-two. Stanley described the initial rapids as a "watery hell", and later confessed:

There is no fear that any other explorer will attempt what we have done in the cataract region. It will be insanity in a successor. Nor would we have ventured on this terrible task, had we the slightest idea that such fearful impediments were before us.

Stanley devised a system of attaching rattan (a strong flexible vine) hawsers to the boats to hold them back from the rapids, with teams of men holding them from the banks. When this didn't work, the canoes had to be manhandled along the shore, often over jagged and slippery rocks and boulders. Often the hawsers would be ripped from the hands of fifty men, and the canoes swept to destruction. He described the Father rapid thus:

The Father is the wildest stretch of river I have ever seen. Take a strip of sea blown over by a hurricane, four miles in length and half a mile in breadth, and a pretty accurate conception of its leaping waves may be obtained. The roar was tremendous and deafening. I can only compare it to the thunder of an express train through a rock tunnel... The most powerful ocean steamer, going at full speed on this portion of the river, would be as helpless as a cockleboat.

Many men were lost in the raging torrents, and later downriver when the rattan hawsers controlling his English boat *Lady Alice* were ripped from the hands of the men on the bank, his craft was swept into the middle of the river. Stanley was almost drowned himself:

We rode downwards furiously on the crests of proud waves... Never did rocks assume such hardness, such solemn grimness and bigness, never were they invested with such terrors and such grandeur... The flood was resolved that we should taste the bitterness of death... We saw the river heaved bodily upward, as though a volcano was about to belch around us... I shouted out, "Pull men, for your lives."

By this time, his companion Frank Pocock was crippled with foot ulcers, and when they could not travel by boat, he had to be carried in a litter along the shore. On one stretch of rapids called Zinga Falls, Stanley went ahead to make a reconnaissance. His orders to the remaining men were that the canoes could shoot the rapids where safe, but to portage when it was not safe, and Frank was to be carried the entire way overland on his litter. After Stanley had left, Frank countermanded the order and had the men lift him into a canoe, but after successfully running one rapid they came to a booming cataract and the boatmen pulled in. They said it was too dangerous to run, but Frank refused to be carried around and insisted they run it. He eventually called the boatmen cowards for not daring to attempt it, and goaded beyond endurance, one of the boatmen turned to the others and said:

"Boys, our little master is saying we are afraid of death. I know there is

death in the cataract, but come, let us show him that black men fear death as little as white men."

The canoe was re-launched, and observers remarked:

There was a greasy slipperiness about the water that was delusive, and it was irresistibly bearing them broadside over the falls… Roused from his seat by the increasing thunder of the fearful waters, Frank rose to his feet, and looked over the heads of those in front, and now the full danger of the situation burst on him. But it was too late! They had reached the fall, and plunged headlong amid the waves and spray. The angry waters rose and leapt into their vessel, and spun them around to the whirlpools, which yawned below. Ah! Then came the moment of anguish, regret and terror.

Frank's body was found eight days later washed up on the bank.

When Stanley finally reached the treacherous Isangila cataracts, he decided to abandon the boats, and head overland. The locals had told him that Boma was only five days march away, and for three days they struggled forward through the cruel, punishing Crystal Mountains. On the fourth day Stanley called a halt, the party was finished and people were dying. He wrote a letter and asked for volunteers to take it ahead to Boma. It read:

To any gentleman who speaks English at Boma

Dear Sir,

I have arrived at this place from Zanzibar with 115 souls, men, women and children. We are now in a state of imminent starvation. We can buy nothing from the natives, for they laugh at our cloth, beads and wire… I do not know you; but I am told there is an Englishman at Boma, and as you are a Christian and a gentleman, I beg you not to disregard my request.

A couple of days later, a well-provisioned caravan returned, and after a day of feasting, Stanley set off for Boma. On the ninth of August 1877, the 999th day since leaving Zanzibar, he was greeted by four white men, three Portuguese and a Dutchman. He initially refused to be carried in their hammock, but when they said it was a Portuguese custom, he finally agreed. He had come 7000 miles through the Dark Continent, to be carried the final steps into Boma.

★ ★ ★

I was told to stay away from the Angolan side of the river, but couldn't help myself stopping for a leak there, as there didn't seem to be anybody about. Five minutes later I noticed a tiny red flag flying over a small stone hut, and no sooner did I change course for the Congo side than two guys jumped into a dugout canoe and gave chase shouting something which sounded like Portuguese. They didn't seem to have guns, so I just put the power on and didn't look back. They soon gave up. Just as I arrived in Boma, a massive container ship passed from behind nearly capsizing me in its wake.

A century ago, Boma was an important staging post on route to Matadi, and today it's still a busy port. I decided to treat myself, and spend the night in a hotel conveniently situated right by the river. It had an extended balcony built on stilts over the water, where part of the restaurant was situated. Whilst the guests were drinking cold beer and tucking into their fine cuisine above, I was paddling between the stilts beneath, dodging the crabs. They looked pretty shocked when I climbed over the wall onto the balcony, looking like a drowned rat.

As comfortable and enjoyable as the hotel was, before I arrived I noticed a ramshackle looking village just before it. After I had dragged up my canoe and settled into the hotel, I decided to go and check it out.

The contrast here between rich and poor fully hit home when I did so. It actually turned out to be a market with people living in mud huts either side of the main street. By street, I mean a five-foot wide walkway, trodden and worn into the mud about two feet deep. Luckily it was dry, and either side of this path were numerous wooden tables made from branches and driftwood. But most impressive was the variety of food on offer.

A huge wild boar, blood still dripping from its slit throat was on one table, and alongside it a similarly intact antelope, its hairy flanks glistening in the sun. Another table was awash with a multitude of wild mushrooms, none of which I recognised, unsurprisingly. Then there were clusters of live crabs tied together, river snails and a variety of what seemed to be ants and termites, some of which were coated in honey. As an aperitif to the cold beer and chicken and chips I planned to have later, I selected a roasted fruit bat from a pile. Funnily enough it was disgusting, and I didn't eat it all.

★ ★ ★

I chatted to some of the locals in the hotel and they had all agreed that the headwinds would be too strong for me to paddle against from here to the mangroves, and sure enough the next day it was blowing a gale. It was only a forty-five minute motorboat ride to the shelter of the mangrove swamps of Muanda Marine Reserve, and that, along with the fact that my flight to Kinshasa was booked in two days time, persuaded me to hitch a lift to the village of Malela at the entrance to the swamps. An Angolan called Mee Mee found a boat that was leaving that morning. I padded into a busy little harbour, and the whole place erupted as they realised there was a white bloke in there midst. To save myself getting mobbed I just hung off the shore hoping to catch a glimpse of my Angolan friend.

Eventually he showed up, the crowds parted and I loaded my canoe onto a boat not much bigger than mine. After waiting for a couple of hours, and allowing six more people to get in, the owner suddenly demanded twice the agreed fee. I just laughed and ignored him, but he kept on and on and on, and only when I untied my canoe and started to drag it off did he get the message and give in. I felt a bit guilty getting a lift, but even with a fifty horsepower outboard engine the boat was having a hard time ploughing into the relentless headwind. We were all soaked by the time we arrived at Malela, a village on the edge of the mangroves. It was mid afternoon. My final destination of Banana and the Atlantic Ocean was a mere ten miles away, but because the tide was coming in it made sense to wait till the next morning.

Malela was situated on an island at the entrance to the Mangrove swamps, and was truly unique. To prevent everything and everybody from sinking into the mud, the entire village was built on a foundation of millions of discarded mussel, clam and oyster shells. All the buildings were built from bamboo, and the entire economy funnily enough, depended on harvesting, boiling and selling mussels, clams and oysters.

It all felt a bit wild west for the first half hour or so; quite a few soldiers, lots of whispering and wild eyed staring. But after an English-speaking guy by the name of Philip (a fine name) turned up, things started to relax a little. When he told everybody I had just spent five months paddling the Congo River I became an instant celebrity, and I was summoned inland down a little mussel shell path to the main village encampment. It turned out Philip was the immigration officer of the village and had five soldiers and two other immigration guys working with him. They couldn't have been more welcoming.

For months I had been thinking about what to do with my canoe at the end of the trip. I couldn't afford to fly it home, and I had entertained the idea of giving it away, but another option was to get somebody to look after it for me. Then when I had the money, I would return for another canoe expedition down the Zambezi River, the source of which wasn't a million miles away in Angola.

But after meeting the chief, I felt the right thing to do was to give something back to the fishermen who had helped me out so much during the trip. As he was such a lovely old character, and reminded me of my granddad, I decided to give him the canoe. After Philip got over the shock of my announcement, and explained what I had said to the chief, his face lit up like a Christmas tree and I felt a warm glow inside. Maybe I wasn't such heartless bastard after all. I was given my own hut for the night and taken on a tour of the village.

The shore was awash with groups of guys coaxing open fires, on top of which were half oil drums full of fresh mussel shells boiling away, with a little blanket placed over the top to steam them. When they were ready, they were piled up while some other guys took them out of their shells. Lastly they were skewered onto bamboo sticks where they were taken to sell in Boma or Banana.

They even had a purpose built bar (when beer was available) and as it was my last night on the river, I bought the chief and a few of the guys a warm beer as the sun went down.

"What's it like living here?" I asked the chief. "Are you ever affected by any of the fighting further inland?"

"I've been here thirty-two years," he said, clearly enjoying his beer. "We are away from all the fighting, nobody ever bothers us here. We can go to Angola whenever we want, we have no passports, it is a safe place."

Tucked away amongst a multitude of tidal mangrove islands in an estuary ten miles wide, you could see why. It wasn't exactly of political significance.

"How much did you pay for your canoe, and why do you want to give it to me?" he asked.

He looked so humble. I knew I had made the right decision. His gentle smile revealed his missing lower front teeth, and though he walked with a limp, he looked pretty healthy for what I imagined must have been around sixty years old.

"I bought the canoe for about thirteen hundred US dollars." They all looked at each other in disbelief. "But its not worth that now," I quickly added. "It's a good canoe, it's fast, very tough, and if you look after it, it will last twenty years easy."

"Why do you want to give it to us?" he asked again.

I noticed he had said us and not me: another reason to think he was the right guy.

"Of all the people I have met in the last five months, it is the fishermen who have helped me the most," I said and he nodded his head in approval. "Others have threatened to kill me, tried to rob me," I said, making the 'cut throat' sign with my hand across my throat. "But, I honestly don't think I would have made it this far, if I hadn't had the help from the fishermen along the way: people like you."

The next morning, the whole village seemed to have turned out to say goodbye. One of whom happened to be Philip's wife; a real beauty with a drop dead gorgeous smile. I was so mesmerised I couldn't take my eyes off her, and it actually became a little bit embarrassing as I just stood and stared. I was in love with another man's wife. However, as was the story of my life, it was not to be. As I got ready to leave, my love life quickly reverted to the familiar barren wasteland, complete with tumbleweed.

The time had finally come for the last day of my journey, with a measly ten miles to go until my obsession would finally come to an end at the Atlantic Ocean. The chief had supplied the best fisherman in the village, Louis, to show me the way through the Mangrove swamp, and he was then going to tow my canoe back to the village afterwards. His eyes looked in different directions and he wore a white knee length doctor's coat, but he knew the swamp like the back of his hand. Apparently these swamps were home to crocodiles, hippos and manatee, the big fat sea cow creatures. Although they weren't supposed to be hunted here, this was the Congo and these people needed to feed their kids.

I'd have been lost in ten minutes flat trying it on my own. Channels disappeared off in all directions; sometimes we were paddling against the current and sometimes going with the flow. We only stopped once, during a rainstorm, in a crab fishing settlement on stilts, where Louis's mate made us a hot drink. If I thought the 'mussel shell' village was poor, this place beat it hands down. But what really left its mark was the host's disability. His right arm was literally skin and bone and completely withered, but without help from the outside he had been forced to simply get on with it and make a life for himself. He still paddled his canoe everyday setting and checking his crab pots. He had a wife and kid to support, and lived in the middle of a swamp surrounded by mud. I gave him all the food I had left, my pots and a few other bits and bobs.

It only took us four hours to get to Banana, which was situated on a tiny spit of land no wider than a couple of hundred metres across. On the other side was the Atlantic Ocean. Just before we arrived a police boat had insisted I go to the immigration office straight away, but when I finally hit the beach and handed everything over to Louis, apart from letting out a whoop of joy that turned heads, I had other things on my mind. The last thing I wanted to do was go to the immigration office.

After I said my farewells to Louis and handed him my paddle, I climbed straight over a five feet wall directly onto the coast road and stuck my thumb out. No sentiment about leaving my trusty canoe that had served me so well. I had done it, and thank Christ for that! I was looking at the Atlantic Ocean, waves crashing onto the beach. To the far left I could see the Angolan coastline, and the gap in the mangroves where the main channel opened out into the sea, and just offshore were some islands, probably Angolan. To the right, the narrow beach disappeared off into the distance and you could just make out some high ground a couple of miles away.

At last my obsession had been laid to rest. I had got it all out of my system. I didn't need to suffer anymore. I could now revert to a normal life with a steady girlfriend, a mortgage and settle down in a friendly community somewhere in the Welsh mountains...

Or maybe not.

The reality was that adventurous expeditions were in my blood, and in the last couple of months I had already been contemplating paddling the Zambezi from source to sea, or even the Lomani (in the Congo). And of course I still wanted to sea kayak around Ireland, canoe across Canada living off the land, build a log cabin in Alaska: there were so many brilliant trips to do out there and only one lifetime to do it all in. What I really needed was a flexible highly paid outdoor job, with a crazy girlfriend obsessed with wild places.

The next town a couple of miles up the coast was Muanda, where I had my flight booked the next morning, and right on the beach was a French owned bar with a couple of expats having a beer.

"You're lucky to be alive. These people are not like you and me," said a guy called Pierre after we exchanged pleasantries. He clicked his fingers impatiently at the Congolese bartender. "Beer!" he ordered, tapping the bar with his uncooked sausage of a finger.

Unsurprisingly the rest of him was also pale and fat, not in itself a reason to dislike him, but combined with his rude behaviour and ridiculous safari outfit... Well, I couldn't help but think he was a prick. His wallet was as fat as he was too.

"You have to understand," he continued. "These people are not civilised. They cannot help themselves."

Even with a powerful fan whirling away on the ceiling above him, he was still sweating heavily. I imagined the damage the fan would do if it were to fall on his head.

"There's good and bad in every country," I eventually replied. "And besides, the fisherman here could teach us a thing or two."

"What could the fishermen possibly teach us?" Pierre laughed.

I wanted to say, "You wouldn't understand you ignorant bastard."

"Humility," I suggested eventually.

He mumbled something under his breath before returning to his beer.

His attitude seemed quite typical of some expats out here. Living in compounds behind razor wire fences, and driving around in chauffeur driven, air-conditioned land cruisers, they were cut off from reality. And because they had so much security, I believe they developed a paranoia and mistrust of the locals. Even though I had experienced a fair amount of hostility, I still believed the majority of the people were good.

I had one beer and some food then headed onto the beach to shoot my final piece for my film. I found a quiet spot with the waves lapping the shore and set up my video camera and tripod. Just as I began to pour my heart out, a rotund looking soldier appeared from nowhere and came wandering over to investigate. Here we go again. I was in such a great mood, it was the last day of the trip, and I was ecstatic. Please, please don't let soldier boy ruin my day.

"You can't film here, show me your papers," he said.

How did I know he was going to say that? I didn't handle it very well. I explained that I'd just spent five months canoeing the Congo River, and that I was just filming the last day, that the camera was only showing me, the beach and the ocean, that I'd be done in five minutes and then I'd fly out tomorrow and he'd never see me again.

"You can't film here, show me your papers," he continued with a deadpan expression.

"I am filming here, and if that means burying you up to your neck in the sand me old mate then so be it," I thought.

I showed him my filming permit and my passport, which he rudely grabbed from my hand before carefully scrutinising them. He cut to the chase: "Give me money."

I instinctively snatched my documents out of his hand – at which point he instinctively grabbed my camera – at which point I grabbed him by his lapels with both hands. I don't think either of us expected that to happen. Grabbing my camera had been like a red rag to a bull and I unleashed a torrent of abuse and threats at him with my face inches from his.

"Give me my fucking camera back!" I screamed.

Five months of fatigue and frustration had again found a release onto this unfortunate victim, and I think he realised he was dealing with an unhinged Mondele.

He eventually gave it back, at about the same time as his officer turned up out of nowhere. On hearing my story and seeing my papers, and being the man that he was, he let me carry on and took bullyboy away – to my great relief. The last thing I would have needed was to be locked up on the last day.

★ ★ ★

The next morning I flew in to Kinshasa on a bush plane so small I could have strangled the pilot without taking my seatbelt off. Ironically, he must have been using the Congo River as a navigational aid, and I had some great views of the cataracts and rapids below. Even though we were a few thousand feet up, in places the river was completely white, and you could even see some of the enormous re-circulating boils. I now didn't feel too bad about having missed this section out.

I nearly had a fight with a baggage handler at Kinshasa airport, who didn't want to give me my bag back until I gave him some money. Then, when I tried to leave the airport on foot so as not to get ripped off by the taxis, I got even more grief from the porters who get commission; or not in my case.

The day after that, I took an Air France flight out of the Congo. As the plane took off I let out an audible sigh of relief, releasing a sound not unlike the one you hear when somebody dies in a film. It was over, and I didn't have to be an on the edge, paranoid, schizophrenic nutter anymore. In all my life, I don't think I've ever come as close to a nervous breakdown as I had on this trip.

On the plus side, I had achieved what I set out to do. More importantly, I had been privileged to experience the best and the worst of human nature, both with the local people and in my own behaviour. These lessons alone were well worth any hardships I may have encountered. I also hoped that I'd never complain about anything, ever again.

On reflection, the Democratic Republic of the Congo is an incredibly interesting and diverse country to visit, especially if you go off the beaten track. But if you go there with a fixed agenda and on your own, you need to be prepared to take a chill pill. The people are both brave and inspirational, and if you think about the amount of turmoil they have been through in the past, you can't really blame them for the occasional hostile act.

I've always been hugely impressed by people who have overcome adversity. Whatever adversity that is, when things become very difficult, there comes a crucial tipping point where a decision needs to be made about whether to carry on or not. Whether to hang in there or give up, whether to maintain the moral high ground or let things slide. I would suggest that the outcome depends almost exclusively on strength of character. Janvier, the brothers and the majority of the Congolese I had met had this quality in abundance. Unfortunately for them, with an inept government, they didn't have much opportunity to channel their courage and determination into building a comfortable and more successful life for themselves. The tragedy is, given the opportunity other countries possess, these incredibly hard working and courageous people might achieve anything they set their minds to.

EPILOGUE

On my return, I had planned to continue working for Outward Bound as an instructor. I did some freelance work for them, but soon realised there was something missing. Although there were occasional disadvantaged students coming to us, the majority of our clients were from relatively comfortable backgrounds. It then dawned on me that my outlook had changed.

Due to my experience in the Congo, I now had more respect for disadvantaged youth than privileged youth. They were harder work, more stressful and gave me more grief, but I felt these guys needed my help more.

Although I missed the mountains, I left Outward Bound and joined the charity Fairbridge in inner city London. I was now working as a development trainer with the hardest-to-reach young people London had to offer, and I have to say it was a lot more satisfying. Like the Congolese, some of these young people had almost lost hope, and hearing their stories was often heartbreaking. But day in day out I would recognise the same admirable qualities, derived from overcoming adversity.

Ironically, and this too was reminiscent of the Congo I was often verbally abused, intimidated and even received death threats. But to do my job properly, I needed to believe in these people. In many ways, I actually believe these youngsters had an advantage over more privileged young people. Due to the constant struggle of their lives, they had more opportunity to develop courage, determination and strength of mind than a youngster from a loving family, possibly spoilt, and with no need to struggle. I once even had an asylum seeker from Kinshasa turn up, and guess what? He was the hardest working lad in the group.

★ ★ ★

Inspired by the thought of paddling other rivers in the Congo, I had previously urged Janvier to get an email address set up in Kisangani. I also promised him that whenever I got out of debt (from this trip), I'd send him some money to help with his pharmacy business. He did send me an email six months later, but unfortunately I was still up to my neck in debt at that time. Since then I've lost contact.

A year after my return, I was very grateful to receive my Winston Churchill Memorial Trust Fellowship medal. The Duchess of Cornwall (Camilla) presented the award at the Guild Hall in London, and although I wore a jacket and tie, I was the only person to wear jeans. (I didn't own a pair of trousers.) I was also very honoured to be awarded the 2008 Mike Jones Canoeing Award. Mike Jones was one of the most well known expedition kayakers of his era, and led the 1976 kayak expedition down the Dudh Kosi River from Mount Everest. He tragically drowned whilst trying to rescue a companion on the Braldu River in Pakistan in 1978, and the Winston Churchill Memorial Trust now administers the award along with his sister.

My documentary film of the trip won Best Feature at the Llanberis Mountain Film Festival and was runner up at the Sheffield Adventure Film Festival. It's also gone on show around the United States, as part of the Vancouver International Mountain Film Festival's Best of Festival tour.

The film is available to buy on my website
www.canoeingthecongo.com

WINSTON
CHURCHILL
MEMORIAL
TRUST

The Winston Churchill Memorial Trust operates a Travelling Fellowship scheme which awards grants to enable British Citizens from all walks of life to travel overseas to acquire knowledge for the benefit of their profession and community, the UK as a whole, and themselves.

The 10 annual categories cover a wide variety of topics from the arts and crafts, rural affairs and the environment, to industry, technology, sport, young people, social concerns, and exploration.

As well as promoting the ideal of understanding between peoples, the travel experience makes Churchill Fellows more effective at work and in their community. Over 100 grant awards are made annually with an average duration abroad of 4-8 weeks.

Winston Churchill Memorial Trust
29 Great Smith Street (South Door)
London
SW1P 3BL
Tel: 020 7799 1660
Fax: 020 7799 1667
office@wcmt.org.uk

THE
OUTWARD
BOUND TRUST

The Outward Bound Trust was founded in 1941 by Lawrence Holt, Chairman of the Blue Funnel Shipping Line, and the renowned educationalist Kurt Hahn. It was intended as a survival school for merchant seamen who might find themselves shipwrecked and forced to cope with all manner of situations and conditions in any environment in the world.

After the war, it was felt by many that the success of the school was in more than just teaching survival skills. The Outward Bound programme could also, in peacetime, be a valuable means of making individuals more independent, self aware and able to cope for themselves. The lessons learned have, from the start, been applied to teamwork and leadership.

ENQUIRIES / HEAD OFFICE
Hackthorpe Hall
Hackthorpe
Penrith
Cumbria CA10 2HX
Tel: 01931 740000   Fax: 01931 740001
Email: enquiries@outwardbound.org.uk

APPENDIX

ADVICE & EQUIPMENT
 Stanford Maps
12 – 14 Long Acre
London
WC2E 9LP
www.stanfords.co.uk
020 7836 1321

Nomad Travel & Medical
3 – 4 Wellington Terrace
Turnpike Lane
London
N8 0PX
www.nomadtravel.co.uk
020 8889 7014

Royal Geographical Society
1 Kensington Gore
London
SW7 2AR
www.rgs.org
020 7591 3000

OUTDOOR SKILLS PROVIDERS

North Wales Active – www.northwalesactive.co.uk
Plas Y Brenin – www.pyb.co.uk
Plas Menai – www.plasmenai.co.uk
Glenmore Lodge – www.glenmorelodge.org.uk